Mrs Ronnie

the society hostess who collected kings

Mrs Ronnie

the society hostess who collected kings

by

Siân Evans

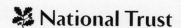
National Trust

For my parents, Rae and David

First published in the United Kingdom in 2013 by
National Trust Books
10 Southcombe Street
London W14 0RA

An imprint of Anova Books Company Ltd

ISBN: 9781907892387

A CIP catalogue record for this book is available from the British Library.

20 19 18 17 16 15 14 13
10 9 8 7 6 5 4 3 2 1

Reproduction by Mission Productions Ltd, Hong Kong
Printed and bound by Toppan Leefung Printing, China

This book can be ordered direct from the publisher at the website:
www.anovabooks.com, or try your local bookshop. Also available from
National Trust shops and www.shop.nationaltrust.org.uk

Previous page: **The
Honourable Mrs Ronald
Greville, photographed
in 1900 by the Lafayette
Studio of Bond Street.**

Contents

Introduction

'Mrs Ronnie of Polesden Lacey' was a shrewd social climber, an ardent collector of royalty, a rigorous businesswoman, an inveterate traveller and a mercurial philanthropist with some controversial political beliefs. She was born Margaret Helen Anderson in 1863, ostensibly the only child of two working-class Scots transplanted to London. However, her lowly origins concealed a fascinating secret, and she used her charm and cunning, not to mention the fortune left to her by the man thought to be her stepfather, to become a close friend of many members of the British Royal Family, and of kings, queens, maharajahs and millionaires from all over the world.

Margaret went by a number of names throughout her life: to her intimate friends she was Maggie or Aunt Maggie; she liked being known to Edwardian society as Mrs Ronnie; and, although she rarely used the title, formally she was known as Dame Margaret Greville, having been awarded the DBE in 1922. In fact, her multiple names are an indication of her frequent metamorphoses. Tough and ambitious, she reinvented herself as it suited her, covering her tracks, and destroying any evidence that might not show her in a good light. Plucked from obscurity by her mother's late marriage, she was quick to leave the Edinburgh lodging house behind; as soon as she was safely married in 1891 to the affable Ronnie Greville, 'Maggie' started to record the edited highlights of her new life in press clippings, now stored in albums in her beautiful country house, Polesden Lacey. Once she had inherited a fortune in her own right, and was widowed, childless and alone at 50 years old, she used her wealth and independence to create a social circle of the powerful and influential, inviting them to her two magnificent houses, where luxury was the watchword.

Tough and ambitious, she reinvented herself as it suited her, covering her tracks, and destroying any evidence that might not show her in a good light.

Left: **Portrait of the Hon. Mrs Ronald Greville (1863–1942), painted in 1891 by Charles Auguste Émile Durand, known as Carolus-Duran (1837–1917).**

Proximity to royalty, starting with Edward VII, became a habit that was hard to break, and her long life encompassed friendships with King George V and Queen Mary, and King George VI and Queen Elizabeth. Her only failure in this field was with the Prince of Wales, the future Edward VIII, of whom she held a low opinion; the feeling was mutual. Needless to say, she was much involved in the Abdication Crisis.

She travelled extensively and always gravitated to the most powerful and influential people of the age, which brought her into contact with Mussolini and Hitler. She also sponsored and supported people of far-sighted intelligence and ability, from inventors such as Marconi and scientists like Professor Lindemann, to major politicians like Sir John Simon and Winston Churchill.

She travelled extensively and always gravitated to the most powerful and influential people of the age, which brought her into contact with Mussolini and Hitler.

She was revered and feared in equal measure, especially by the other society hostesses of the age; adroit at the astute put-down, her voice, with its gentle Edinburgh accent, was described by Prime Minister Balfour as 'a sort of honeyed poison', and she enjoyed getting her retaliation in first. She courted the press, using the media to present herself in the best possible light, but she was also aware that her post-mortem reputation would be damaged by her involvement with the momentous political developments of the 1930s, especially her early misplaced enthusiasm for the Third Reich. Consequently, she left instructions that her private papers should be destroyed by her faithful Head Steward, Francis Bole, who had been loyal to her for four decades.

However, she was not able to suppress all information about her life, much of which was led in a highly public manner and consequently reported in papers, magazines and photographs of her era. Stories about her were also recorded in the diaries, letters and memoirs of her contemporaries, many of them unfavourable. Though she tried to manipulate her own public image, it has been possible to fill the gaps with help and advice from many people who have been extremely generous with their knowledge.

Above: **The east front of Polesden Lacey. The property was promised to a descendant of King George V in 1914, but was bequeathed to the National Trust in 1942.**

'Mrs Ronnie' provoked strong and conflicting reactions amongst her contemporaries. Cecil Beaton, in 1948, described her as '…a galumphing, greedy, snobbish old toad who watered at her chops at the sight of royalty and the Prince of Wales's set, and did nothing for anybody except the rich.' Picture dealer and art adviser Colin Agnew said of her '…she was a true friend, but a terrible enemy.' But Osbert Sitwell, who knew her for nearly 30 years, stated when she died, 'a great number of men and women of a generation younger than herself, as well as her own contemporaries, have lost an irreplaceable friend.'

Mrs Ronnie schemed and manipulated to the very end of her life. She changed her will, going back on an offer she had made to King George V in 1914, to leave Polesden Lacey to his son Bertie, later King George VI. Instead she left it to the National Trust, along with a massive bequest and almost all the contents in memory of her beloved father, William McEwan, with the desire that the house and grounds should be opened to the public. As an impressive consolation prize, however, she left more than 60 pieces of exquisite world-class jewellery to Queen Elizabeth, and these gems are still worn at formal events by members of the Royal Family.

Mrs Ronnie's life began in obscurity in 1863 as a low-caste Victorian in the age of Empire. When it ended, in 1942, she was the best friend of the Queen and King, stubbornly sitting out the Blitz in the very heart of the beleaguered capital city, as Britain fought for its very survival at the height of the Second World War. This is a story of driving ambition; Margaret Greville was certainly no saint and she made some unwise judgements, but she was a complex and fascinating woman who, through her own determination and social mobility, obtained a front-row seat at many of the most momentous events of her era.

Mr McEwan and Mrs Anderson

"…William McEwan MP, the Scottish millionaire, [is] one of the most interesting men in the House of Commons. Widely read and an acute thinker, no one would guess that this quiet, low-voiced man, with the delicate scholar's face, had been the architect of one of the largest fortunes of his time…"

(Glasgow Evening News, *undated, c.1890*)

The ascetic features of William McEwan, MP, Privy Counsellor send an appraising gaze across the dining room at Polesden Lacey. The portrait in oils depicts an elderly man with a long white beard and of slightly Oriental appearance. McEwan had disliked this particular painting, but Margaret Greville had it hung in pride of place, so that even after his death, she could always sense his presence, as she held court at her famous dining table. The point would not have been lost on her sophisticated and wealthy guests. 'All this…', as she once sweepingly described her luxurious life, '*all this…*', was due to the enterprise, energy and business acumen of a taciturn Scot, supposedly her mother's second husband and, as was suspected but unproven at the time, Margaret's natural father.

An ambitious man

William McEwan was the third child of John McEwan, a ship-owner from the port of Alloa in Scotland, born on 16 July 1827. His father died

Left: **The portrait of Mrs Greville's father, William McEwan, was painted in 1900 by Benjamin Constant and now hangs in the Dining Room at Polesden Lacey.**

when he was four years old; his pregnant mother was helped to bring up her five children by her parents, and they paid for William to attend Alloa Academy. By 1843 sixteen-year-old William was working as a clerk at the Alloa Coal Company, recording coal shipments.

Alloa was a thriving coastal town, reliant on brewing, distilling and glass-making. The narrow streets were full of the pungent smells of beer-making and the sounds of coopering and ship-building. Before the Industrial Revolution, the general population drank beer rather than risk their health from drinking the contaminated water, and half of it was home-produced. However, commercial brewing was a growth industry, and the purity of Alloa's water created demand for the products of the town's breweries all over Scotland.

Young William was ambitious, but lacked any clear direction. In 1845 he embarked upon a grim existence as an accounts clerk in Glasgow for £30 a year. When offered a position as a cashier in a textile company in Yorkshire, at a salary of £70 a year, he leapt at the chance. This was William's first visit to England, and he was disillusioned by what he found at Honley, a 'village without society'. He wrote:

"How often have I heard [that] England was a land of comfort. It may be so according to an English notion of the term but I am sure no Scotchman who has been accustomed to live respectably in his own country can say it is so – what wretched hovels they have got to live in...How miserably have I been deceived on the reports about England..."

(William McEwan's notebook, 1847)

Desperate for company, he attended both the Wesleyan and Independent chapels. Ironically, considering the liquid origins of his phenomenal later success, he joined both the Teetotal Society and the Huddersfield Total Abstinence Society, though he celebrated his 21st birthday supper with friends with a bottle of ginger wine.

The brewery

John Jeffrey, William's uncle, who owned the Heriot Brewery in Edinburgh, offered him a five-year apprenticeship, and William moved up to Edinburgh and set about learning the art and science of brewing. In 1856, financed by a £2,000 loan, William McEwan opened a brewery at Fountainbridge in Edinburgh.

Fountain Brewery started modestly; the wages bill for the first week of operation was a mere 16 shillings. When a potential customer called, McEwan sent word to the cooper to 'hammer like blazes' to give the impression they were busy. His first deliveries were made in January 1857. From the outset McEwan oversaw every aspect of the business; twice a day he toured the site. He was also pragmatic, and ardent in his pursuit of a sale – 'Of one thing I can assure you, that no exertion shall be spared on my part to send you an article second to none in the trade', he stated in a letter in 1857.

William McEwan had used geologists to identify the optimum spot for his brewery, securing unlimited supplies of the purest water hundreds of feet below ground from a vast complex of springs. The brewery was near the Union Canal and adjacent to the Caledonian Railway, from which a spur ran straight into the brewery yard. The spreading rail network allowed his beer to be transported all over Britain, and the raw materials (coal, hops and barley) were brought to the brewery by barge or rail. McEwan's beer was sold to outlets all over Western Scotland and the industrial heartland of Tyneside, supplying the mighty workforce of metal-bashers and ship-builders.

There was a market across the British Empire for reliable bottled beers that travelled well, whether up-country in Simla or under the blazing sun of Perth. McEwan's Export Ale and McEwan's Pale Ale were developed expressly to meet these markets. In 1868 the brewery exported 250 shipments overseas, worth £34,000, to the West Indies, India, Australia, New Zealand; wherever there were hot and thirsty sons of Empire, the familiar sight of a bottle of McEwan's ale offered an opportunity, albeit temporary, to lay down 'the white man's burden'.

Business boomed – within four years of its foundation, the firm's annual turnover was more than £40,000, and William was employing more than 150 men and 50 boys by the early 1870s. By 1880, the brewery site covered 12 acres, and in 1889, McEwan converted the business into a limited liability company, with a capital of £1 million, an astonishing sum, worth more than £48 million in today's money. Within 25 years William had created a booming brand whose quality was respected all over the world.

Below: **Fountain Brewery in the early 1900s; the beer was shipped from Edinburgh to markets all over the world.**

A man of affairs

In the mid-1880s, by then in his 50s, this most private of men surprisingly embraced the life of a man of affairs. He did this in three ways: by seeking public office; by becoming a benefactor of Edinburgh's prestigious but cash-strapped university; and by investing in his adopted city's artistic and cultural heritage. As a result, he mingled with the entrepreneurial classes, politicians and the aristocracy, even royalty, gaining an entrée into the most influential circles in the country.

William McEwan stood as a pro-Gladstone Liberal candidate for the newly created Central Division for Edinburgh, winning the seat in the General Election of 1886. He was highly popular with his constituents for fourteen years, and was returned unopposed at the general election of 1895. He supported Home Rule for Ireland and, though not the most vocal of Parliamentarians, he had a reputation for dispensing excellent advice, and was extraordinarily well-connected. As *The New York Times* reported on 23 December 1894:

"Mr McEwan…exerts a tremendous personal influence in the lobby… he is immensely wealthy and scatters his money freely, though with somewhat selfish discrimination. He entertains lavishly and at his London residence, 4 Chesterfield Gardens, he serves what is practically a free luncheon every day during the Parliamentary season. He is a very intimate friend of Lord Rosebery, who is a shareholder in the McEwan brewery…"

In 1900 Mr McEwan retired from politics on the grounds of ill-health; at the subsequent election for his seat, the unsuccessful candidate was Arthur Conan Doyle, creator of Sherlock Holmes. Mr McEwan declined a peerage from Edward VII in 1907, saying, 'I would rather be first in my own order, than be at the tail end of another.' However, he was delighted by the greater accolade of being appointed Privy Councillor the same year, a rare honour. William McEwan was Deputy Lieutenant of Edinburgh for 30 years, a position which brought him into contact with visiting royalty, and it may have been in this capacity that he first encountered the Prince of Wales, later to become Edward VII, who was to hold the taciturn Scot in high regard for his financial acumen.

'I would rather be first in my own order, than be at the tail end of another.'

William McEwan's second career in politics ran concurrently with his philanthropy to the City of Edinburgh. His notebooks and diaries record his previous small, discreet gifts to charities, and he supported a number of good causes throughout his career. But in the mid-1880s McEwan seems to have decided to make his philanthropy more public.

The University boasted a highly respected medical school, and 'Edinburgh men' were well regarded as surgeons and physicians worldwide. However, it lacked a formal graduation hall in which to bestow its degrees; indeed, there was no building in Edinburgh that could accommodate more than 3,000 people for lectures, presentations or concerts. William McEwan curtailed the civic hand-wringing by offering to fund the entire construction of the building, and work began in 1889. Neo-classical in design, the McEwan Hall is semi-circular and has two ranks of galleried seating in the manner of a theatre. The interior of the hall was decorated with vast wall paintings in the style of the early Renaissance.

The McEwan Hall was formally opened on 3 December 1897. It represented a huge investment in both the University and the City of Edinburgh by one of its least publicity-hungry residents. The whole project cost £115,000 (more than £6.8 million today). Mr McEwan was given an honorary Law degree and his philanthropy was held up to shame the less open-handed:

"...surely it is no small reproach to our modern civilisation that men like Mr McEwan are so rare. In a society where rich men, and even exceedingly rich men, are so numerous as in ours such generosity as his ought not to be exceptional or particularly remarkable..."

(The Times, *4 December 1897*)

Meanwhile, McEwan was keen to establish his credentials as a man of culture; largely self-taught, he went to the Great Exhibition of 1851, on his first trip to London, and he also visited the great country house of Chatsworth. On business trips to Holland, he saw some of Rembrandt's paintings, and he developed a well-informed taste for the Dutch Old Masters. McEwan bought Franz Hals's *Dutch Lady* and *Dutch Gentleman* for the National Gallery of Scotland in 1885, his first recorded purchases of art, and in 1892 he gave £5,775 for Rembrandt's *Woman in Bed*, which he donated to the same gallery. By the 1890s McEwan was collecting Dutch paintings, particularly seascapes and marine themes, perhaps an echo of his youth in Alloa. His most important private purchases, such as *The Golf-players* by Pieter de Hooch, which was painted around 1660, were left to Margaret Greville on his death.

It seems that Mr McEwan's burst of public activity and serious expenditure in the 1880s was due to young Margaret and her mother, Helen. On 26 November 1885, the bachelor Mr McEwan quietly married the widow Mrs Anderson, with her daughter 'M.H. Anderson' as a witness. They chose the discreet anonymity of St Peter's in unfashionable Pimlico, in London, rather than risking the prurient scrutiny of Edinburgh society, where they lived. Helen Anderson was nearly 50 years old, a former lodging house-keeper, and her new husband was 58. However, this unlikely romance, between one of Edinburgh's leading entrepreneurs and wealthy public figures, and a pretty but stout bombazine-clad lady of humble origins, was no sudden infatuation.

This unlikely romance, between one of Edinburgh's leading entrepreneurs and wealthy public figures, and a pretty but stout bombazine-clad lady of humble origins, was no sudden infatuation.

William McEwan and Helen Anderson

Helen Anderson was born in Dunfermline in 1837, to Thomas and Helen Lawrence Anderson. Her father was an agricultural labourer, and as the third of twelve children, she was sent out to work to help support the family. According to the 1861 census, when she would have been 24, Helen had left home; it is most likely that she was 'living in' as a domestic servant in Edinburgh. However, her unmarried older sister Isabella, also a domestic servant, was back at the family home with a three-year-old child, Daniel, and Isabella subsequently had a second illegitimate son, David. It seems that the Andersons were a close family, who would not ostracise an unmarried daughter for having a child.

It is not known how William McEwan met Helen Anderson, but she worked as a servant in Edinburgh, and latterly proved herself to be competent to run a boarding house. Mr McEwan lived in boarding houses all his adult life until his late marriage. It is therefore likely their paths crossed as lodger and servant in the same establishment in the late 1850s or early 1860s.

Close examination of the McEwan's brewery records for the early 1860s reveals a number of male Andersons on the payroll, and a single 'Miss Anderson', who received four payments on a casual basis between August 1862 and June 1863. The name then disappears from the brewery records. Seven months later, January 1864, Helen Anderson's name appears on the birth certificate of her baby, Margaret Helen Anderson, who was born on 20 December 1863. Listed as the father is William Murray Anderson, and it appears that the new baby's parents are living quietly and respectably in London.

The scurrilous story spread in later decades was that Helen was married and her husband, William Anderson, worked as Mr McEwan's day-porter at the brewery. Due to his passion for Helen, Mr McEwan had her husband put on the overnight shift, for his own convenience. The story concluded that the Andersons had subsequently moved to London, and produced a single child, Margaret Helen Anderson, and that Mr Anderson had died while the child was young. This version of events did at least grant Margaret legitimacy, implying that her mother had been married when she was born.

The truth was more complicated and no less intriguing. No marriage record exists for Helen Anderson in England or Scotland, at least not until 1885, but the William Murray Anderson who appeared on the child's birth certificate was married, though not to Helen; he had wed an Ann McPherson in 1852.

Extensive research carried out by Alma Topen from the University of Glasgow Archives has established that William Murray Anderson had been born in Selkirk in 1830 and, by the early 1860s, he was working for Mr McEwan as a cellarman, a position of some trust and responsibility. William Anderson's name is listed in the company records throughout 1862, but there is no record of his name after May 1863 until May 1864, an unexplained gap in a career that subsequently continued unbroken at the brewery for a further three decades.

It is likely that Mr Anderson was taken into his employer's confidence to save Helen's reputation. By dint of his surname, he could provide a convenient cloak of respectability for the pregnant and unmarried Helen, by taking her to London and remaining with her there until the baby was born. This would save the child from the stigma of illegitimacy; the mother could eventually return to her home town, claiming a brief marriage and widowhood in the far-off capital, and – most importantly – the true identity of the father need never be known. Mr McEwan was in a position to fund the venture handsomely, and it appears that the subterfuge was successful.

'Mr and Mrs Anderson' rented 4, Wellington Place, which overlooked Lord's Cricket Ground, and was a pleasant street in an outer suburb of London. Significantly, St John's Wood was a byword for discretion; many of its villas housed the mistresses of wealthy men. Here they awaited the birth of her child; Margaret Helen Anderson arrived on 20 December 1863, and her

Below: **The former 'Mrs' Helen Anderson, following her marriage to Mr McEwan in 1885.**

birth was registered on 8 January 1864 by William Murray Anderson, who stated he was the father, and gave his occupation on the birth certificate as 'commercial traveller'. Helen and William did not need to prove they were married, though the registrar would have assumed that they were, as they had the same surname. The baby was christened on 8 April 1864, and in the baptism records William Murray Anderson's occupation is given as 'gentleman'; a sure sign that he was living on a private source of income.

Helen needed to be absent from Edinburgh for long enough to provide a convincing cover story to account for her baby. Just over a week after Margaret's birth, on 28 December 1863, Helen's father Thomas died in Edinburgh of a 'brain illness', but Helen stayed in London. However, shortly after the baby's christening in London in April 1864, William Anderson returned to his real family, as his name reappears in the brewery account books for May 1864, and he continued in employment there till his death, more than three decades later. Presumably he was well-rewarded for his discretion.

Inevitably, his wife Ann and two older sons were complicit in this secret, as a plausible excuse for his absence was needed for relatives and neighbours. The Andersons' subsequent family life seemed happy enough; Ann gave birth to another son in 1865 and a daughter in 1869; William's two teenage sons still lived at home and his mother-in-law came to live with them too. According to the 1871 census, they were all residing at 107, Fountainbridge. Coincidentally, Helen Anderson's widowed mother, two sisters and two brothers, a nephew and a lodger were also living across the street at 102, Fountainbridge. It is obvious that the two Anderson families knew each other, especially as Thomas, Helen's brother, was a brewer, and the lodger was a brewer's carter.

No death certificate for a William Murray Anderson exists in either England or Scotland between 1863 and 1871; he was, of course, in robust good health and living across the street from his supposed in-laws.

Therefore, a number of people probably knew the truth about Helen Anderson's supposed marriage, but when she returned to Edinburgh at an unknown date, she could pass herself off as a respectable widow, the mother of a little girl whose precise age always remained uncertain. No death certificate for a William Murray Anderson exists in either England or Scotland between 1863 and 1871; he was, of course, in robust good health and living across the street from his supposed in-laws.

Public life and private affairs

On their return to Edinburgh, Mrs Anderson and little Margaret needed a stable income, and it is highly likely that Mr McEwan bankrolled them, as by 1868 Helen was running a lodging house, located at 14, East Maitland Street, where she was employing two servants and providing rooms for three lodgers.

Ironically, William McEwan also resided in lodgings himself; it is interesting to observe the movements of both Helen and William across central Edinburgh, as they rarely lived more than 100 yards from each other and, on one occasion, maintained establishments opposite each other. Helen and Margaret were at East Maitland Street from 1868 until 1875; and Mr McEwan rented rooms at Shandwick Place till 1871, living with his brother John McEwan.

Her efforts to conceal her real age continued all her life; in adulthood, she always claimed to be younger than she actually was...

He then moved to 43, Manor Place, a larger lodging house, where he lived till 1883. His name does not appear in the 1881 census; perhaps he was visiting 4, Atholl Place, a superior establishment nearby, with capacity for ten lodgers, run by Mrs Helen Anderson. Also resident at this address, according to the census, was her daughter Margaret, who had been born in England and was 16 years old in 1881. In fact she was nearly 18; this is the first instance of her 'disguising' her age on official records. Her efforts to conceal her real age continued all her life; in adulthood, she always claimed to be younger than she actually was; her death certificate gave her age as 75, although she was 78, as she had deceived even her own doctor.

Many suspected a long-standing connection between Mr McEwan and 'Mrs' Anderson. This story would remain mere conjecture, were there not primary evidence of their relationship, written in Mr McEwan's own hand, in his private ledger. He had a reputation as a businessman of integrity, and he was a donor to various charitable causes. His private account books prove that he financially supported a 'Mrs Anderson' with half-yearly payments of £14, between November 1874 and May 1877. Payments then appear to stop, although there are substantial withdrawals 'to cash'. Intermittent payments of £14 to Mrs Anderson resume in 1881, and rise to £35 in 1882; meanwhile, Mr McEwan was also paying school fees of roughly £9 a term from October 1878 till January 1884. By 1884 Maggie would have been 20 years old – though, of course, she was supposed to be several years younger than her real age. Similarly, among Mr McEwan's personal papers dating from the late 1870s is a printed flyer that advertises dancing lessons at 'Mr J. Smyth's Academy', with 'November 15th' scrawled in Mr McEwan's hand along one side. It seems highly unlikely that Mr McEwan would have booked a course of dance lessons for himself, but an ability to dance was an essential attribute for genteel young ladies.

In the year 1884–5, William McEwan spent an astonishing £39,671 of his private income on investments and property. Something must have changed this taciturn man's cautious approach to life: he had joined the Liberal party in 1880, had started to live more expansively and was involved in public affairs in Edinburgh. The culmination of this new personality was his marriage to Mrs Helen Anderson in London in 1885, and his decision to stand as a Member of Parliament the following year.

Left: **Marble bust of William McEwan MP by J. Hutchison, signed and dated 1885.**

Having lost his father when he was still a child, William had always been determined to provide for his mother and siblings. His beloved younger brother, John, had died in 1875 in the Royal Edinburgh Asylum after suffering from tuberculosis for twelve years. Their mother passed away in 1879, and his waspish and critical older sister Anne McEwan, an unmarried woman still living in the family home in Alloa and supported by William, died in July 1882 aged 57. It is possible that the deaths of these three close relatives might have relieved McEwan from the shadow of family opprobrium. He was now able to marry the 'unsuitable' Mrs Anderson. Perhaps he was suffering from the Victorian equivalent of a middle-age crisis; more likely, he was finally free to do what he wanted.

The Andersons, mother and daughter, were plucked from respectable obscurity, and suddenly thrust into the public eye, to the delighted horror of Edinburgh society. Mr and Mrs McEwan and Miss Anderson set up house in 25, Palmerston Place, one of the most exclusive new addresses of central Edinburgh. They also acquired a residence in London, 4, Chesterfield Gardens, and the family came to spend most of their time there, perhaps aware of the censure of Scottish high society. The press trod carefully. They universally referred to Miss Anderson as Mr McEwan's 'stepdaughter'; the proprieties were observed in print, no matter how many speculative whispers might be exchanged in Morningside drawing rooms. Osbert Sitwell noted that in later years, the former Miss Anderson took a positive delight in publicly putting down the more genteel Edinburgh matrons; presumably she had endured subtle snubs when younger, and was now in a position to wreak revenge. Robert Bruce Lockhart stated: 'In her new position she could give vent to her likes and dislikes. Edinburgh society, when it visited London, felt the razor-sharp edge of her displeasure.'

'In her new position she could give vent to her likes and dislikes. Edinburgh society, when it visited London, felt the razor-sharp edge of her displeasure.'

Decades later, when she was rich and influential, she carefully tailored stories about her early years, as in the version related by the *Liverpool Post and Mercury*, 14 January 1935: 'Mrs Greville, daughter of the late Mr William McEwan … was brought up quietly in Scotland, but she and her mother made a great social success when they came to London and were honoured with special friendship by King Edward and Queen Alexandra…' At an early age, Margaret had realised the importance of shaping one's own story, and having it disseminated; repeated often enough, it would eventually be taken as the truth. She rarely lied about her origins, but she obscured them, especially the nature of her mother's relationship with the man who was supposed to be her stepfather.

Family was very important to Mr McEwan. In his youth, he had benefited from nepotism and once he was established, he provided for his relatives. Of his four siblings, only his eldest sister Janet had married and produced children. In 1874 he took on his namesake and nephew, William Younger, as an apprentice, and in 1886, when McEwan entered Parliament, William Younger was made the managing director of the Fountain Brewery. It was apparent that William Younger was a businessman of considerable ability; the annual profit between 1885 and 1889 averaged £92,000, and when the company was registered in 1889 as William McEwan & Co., it was reported to be worth £408,000 and had capital of more than £1 million.

All of the ordinary and the bulk of the preference shares were held by McEwan and his family. But despite the business acumen and loyalty of his nephew, it was his 'stepdaughter' Margaret whom McEwan tutored in the Edinburgh office in the intricacies of the business. William and Margaret were close in a way that would have been unlikely if they had really been stepfather and stepdaughter. In addition, looking at the distinctive, almost Oriental features of Mr McEwan and considering Sonia Keppel's acute description of her godmother, Margaret Greville as resembling 'a small Chinese idol with eyes that blinked', one can discern a facial similarity. It is perhaps significant that the worldly Mrs Greville, knowing the truth about her own parentage, often warned, '*Never* remark on a likeness!'

> *Mrs Greville, knowing the truth about her own parentage, often warned, 'Never remark on a likeness!'*

Marriage

"At the present day marriages between young men of ancient family and young women of none are regarded as being highly desirable, provided that the latter has plenty of cash."

(*Ralph Nevill*, English Country House Life, *1925*)

By the late 1880s, Mr McEwan was an extraordinarily influential man; an MP, Deputy Lieutenant for Edinburgh, active philanthropist and astute millionaire. He and his wife, Helen, and her daughter, Margaret, divided their time between the constituency, and their place in central London. He also mixed with the Liberal élite and kept company with some of the most astute men of the age. The small family was moving at the heart of society.

His initial fortune had come from brewing, beer being a commodity so essential in the Victorian era that he had been unable to stop himself from becoming rich, as he freely admitted. He had also invested in the infrastructure and services upon which newly industrialised societies relied – the railways. Mr McEwan became rich at a time when successful entrepreneurs were breaking down many of the class boundaries that had previously existed. Some aristocratic families still shuddered at the prospect of marrying 'trade', but the less fastidious land-owning classes realised by the 1880s that the agricultural depression was eroding the notional value of their holdings and that 'new money' worked just as well as old money in keeping the estates running. Dowager

Left: **Captain the Hon. Ronald Henry Fulke Greville.**

duchesses learned to bite back their comments as the flood of attractive, perfectly groomed American heiresses led the charge.

Mr McEwan, the supposed stepfather of young Margaret Anderson, took an active role in educating her in the ways of business, an unusual attitude for a Victorian entrepreneur. According to Sonia Keppel, Margaret's god-daughter, William McEwan encouraged her 'from her earliest years'. She gradually built up knowledge of the intricate practices and processes of the brewery and its management, and gained considerable business acumen. She learnt to appreciate the power of financial clout through observations in her father's Edinburgh office; in her more mature years, with the McEwan fortune behind her, she expanded her opportunities to wield influence in the drawing rooms and ballrooms of the wealthy and well-connected.

Mr McEwan, through his social connections, came into contact with the Prince of Wales, the future Edward VII, who needed the advice (and, on occasions, the financial assistance) of astute self-made men. The Prince enjoyed the company of the wealthy and was no snob about the source of their fortunes. Indeed, to keep up with the Prince's social circle, with its endless round of race-horse meetings, overseas travel, country house weekends and conspicuous consumption of the very best food, wine, flowers, motorcars, clothes, furs and jewellery, one needed to be very wealthy. It is likely that the millionaire Mr McEwan, renowned for his hospitality and money-making abilities, made it discreetly known that his stepdaughter, Miss Margaret Anderson, would inherit his fortune. His concern was to launch her in society, to use his wealth to establish a secure future for her. The most important aim in any young girl's life was to secure a suitable husband, and a suitable candidate was identified in Ronnie Greville.

Ronnie Greville

The Hon. Ronald Henry Fulke Greville was born on 14 October 1864, the first-born son of the 2nd Baron Greville, Algernon, and his formidable wife, Lady Beatrice Violet Graham, daughter of the 4th Duke of Montrose. Lord Algernon acted as private secretary to Mr Gladstone in 1872 and 1873 and subsequently entered the House of Lords as a Liberal. He also served for a time as groom-in-waiting to Queen Victoria. Ronald, the eldest of four children, was educated at Rugby, and in 1884 he enlisted as a Lieutenant in the 3rd Battalion of the Argyle and Sutherland Highlanders, before transferring to the 1st Life Guards, where he achieved the rank of Captain in 1892.

Affable, well-dressed, well-connected and the heir to a title, Ronald Greville in his twenties was quite a catch. He was part of the Marlborough House Set, the rather louche social circle around the Prince of Wales. With his passion for horses, steeple-chasing, gambling and fine living, Ronnie was a natural pal of the Prince's. However, this lifestyle was expensive; he was well aware that he had to marry a wealthy woman, as the income

Right: Royal Visit (1884) by Henry Hetherington Emmerson. The Prince of Wales, later Edward VII, at Cragside, home of Sir William Armstrong, armaments manufacturer.

from the family estates was surprisingly low, due to the agricultural depression. While the Grevilles had huge holdings of land, mostly in Ireland, they were short of ready cash. What they needed was an amenable heiress, and in the late 1880s Ronnie thought he had found one. Virginia Daniel Bonynge was the stepdaughter and only heir of William Bonynge, a wealthy Californian gold-miner and financier. Virginia came with a dowry of US $4 million, nearly £1 million, but there was a catch. Despite the fact that she was rich, beautiful and good-natured, her father was locked in a vendetta with a former business associate, and the fight became so ugly and so public on both sides of the Atlantic that the Greville family decided against the marriage.

A bizarre and vicious campaign of hatred was conducted between Charles Bonynge and John Mackay, another Californian self-made millionaire, from 1888 till 1892. Both sides engaged agents to publicise the other's lowly origins and boorish behaviour. It was even alleged that Mrs Bonynge was an adulterous bigamist, whose husband was an inmate of San Quentin Prison, and that Virginia Bonynge had a murderer for a father. Their enmity climaxed in a violent fist fight between Mackay and Bonynge in 1891 at the Nevada Bank in San Francisco, and both protagonists, each around 60 years old, fought like tigers till they could be separated by the bank staff. The encounter was reported with some relish in the press:

"Mr Mackay struck when Mr Bonynge was not looking. Then they had it. Chairs turned over, inkstands flew and the ink made long, black streaks on the wall. It was a regular possum and wildcat fight. President Heilman said ,'Gentleman! Gentlemen! This will never do!'"

(Lewiston Daily Sun, *20 January 1891*)

More significantly, as the same paper reported in January 1891: 'Two seasons ago [Virginia] was reported engaged to the Hon. Ronald Greville, only son [sic] of Lord Greville. Some difficulties arose as to settlements … consequently the project fell through, and Greville has since secured another heiress…' It seems the vendetta had deterred the Grevilles, and Ronnie had been encouraged to look for an heiress from a less hazardous social milieu. Ronald had broken off the relationship with Virginia and in seeking a bride with a similarly wealthy stepfather but a less volatile background, he found Margaret Helen Anderson.

The meeting

With heavy-lidded eyes and always immaculately dressed, Ronald Greville was quite a dandy. George Keppel, his best friend from childhood, described him as 'a charming, unambitious man', whom 'Maggie moulded affectionately into any shape she pleased'. Ronald was reported as being 'witty, good-natured, typically Irish', and Margaret would not have tolerated a bore, being intelligent, resourceful and lively in nature herself. Their marriage may have originated in the subtle trade-off between respectable land-owning title and a freshly made fortune, but it was a happy and affectionate relationship. George Keppel said that Margaret was devoted to Ronnie and if they had been able to have children, she would have given up a great deal of her busy social life to care for them.

Ronald was reported as being 'witty, good-natured, typically Irish', and Margaret would not have tolerated a bore, being intelligent, resourceful and lively in nature herself.

It is not certain precisely when and how Ronald and Margaret met, but Ronnie's father, Lord Greville, had been Mr Gladstone's Private Secretary and moved in high Liberal circles, as did Mr McEwan. However, it may just have been a matter of proximity; in the late 1880s Lord and Lady Greville's London address was 7, Chesterfield Gardens; Mr and Mrs McEwan and their daughter resided at number 4. Social etiquette demanded that the respective mothers called on each other, and an initial acquaintance between the two neighbouring households was probably made that way.

They also moved in the same Court circles. Ronald's mother, Lady Violet Greville, described her son as '… a great favourite of … King Edward'. Though mentions of her 'rise without trace' have been deliberately expunged, it seems that Margaret Anderson was launched on the drawing rooms of London's High Society and the periphery of the Prince of Wales's social circle in the late 1880s through her father having extricated the future king from a number of 'financial jams'. Inviting presentable daughters to social events where they might make a good match was part of the deal. Certainly, the fact that Mr McEwan's stepdaughter was to be the only heir to his considerable fortune opened many a salon door for her.

In addition, Mr and Mrs McEwan entertained the great and good at their London house, and Mrs McEwan's 'splendid hospitality' was often remarked on in the press.

By the late 1880s gossip columnists were linking the Grevilles with the McEwans and Miss Anderson. In 1889 Mr and Mrs McEwan and Miss Anderson were staying at the Hotel Prince des Galles in Menton, near Nice. Coincidentally, so was 'The Hon. Ronald Fulke Greville of the Prince of Wales' set…' In winter 1890 a gossip column from the Casino at Monte Carlo lists the affluent guests, including 'Mr and Mrs McEwan and Miss Anderson… and Mr Ronald Greville, 1st Life Guards…' Having struck up an acquaintance in London, their existing friendship flourished when their paths crossed again overseas.

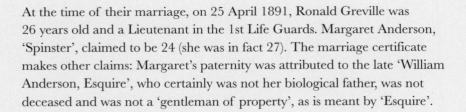

At the time of their marriage, on 25 April 1891, Ronald Greville was 26 years old and a Lieutenant in the 1st Life Guards. Margaret Anderson, 'Spinster', claimed to be 24 (she was in fact 27). The marriage certificate makes other claims: Margaret's paternity was attributed to the late 'William Anderson, Esquire', who certainly was not her biological father, was not deceased and was not a 'gentleman of property', as is meant by 'Esquire'.

It is interesting to speculate on how many of the *dramatis personae* were aware of the true facts; Lord and Lady Greville did not believe that their personable new daughter-in-law was the only child of a deceased manual labourer from Selkirk. Presumably they were also aware that Margaret would eventually inherit Mr McEwan's immense fortune, not for reasons of sentimentality, but because of the stronger ties of blood. Margaret Anderson might not be a member of the peerage but she was certainly one of 'the beerage', the new class whose daughters were successfully marrying into older families. Her antecedents may have lacked grandeur, but any attrition caused by her clamber up the social ladder could be soothed by a poultice of money.

A society wedding

"Bacchus and Ariadne! What a show there was of fine folk and fine feathers on Saturday last at the military wedding on North Audley Street, when Mr Ronald Greville led from the hymeneal altar Miss Margaret Anderson, the stepdaughter of Mr W. McEwan, M.P. for Edinburgh. The weather was tolerably fine, which means that it did not rain and spoil the show; but it was Oh! So cold!…"

(Country Gentleman, *undated*)

The earliest album of press clippings at Polesden Lacey contains various accounts of Maggie and Ronnie's wedding, linked by an undercurrent of speculation about wealth. All concur that at 2pm on Saturday 25 April 1891, the church of St Mark's in Mayfair was adorned with palms and white flowers, and that the congregation was in the very vanguard of fashion, with latecomers hurrying into the church mere seconds before the carriage bearing the bride and her stepfather pulled up at the steps. One small page, a Master Parker, was in cream-coloured satin, and carried a sword. Many remarked on the charm of the four bridesmaids, two of whom bore the noble surname of Greville. Their dresses were of rose pink satin and each wore a diamond rose, thistle and shamrock brooch, the gift of the bridegroom and a symbol of the union of England, Scotland and Ireland.

> *…the church of St Mark's in Mayfair was adorned with palms and white flowers, and that the congregation was in the very vanguard of fashion…*

The bride ('… a gentle-faced, dark-haired girl …', according to the *Leeds Mercury*) wore a dress of rich white satin, with trimmings of very old Brussels lace, caught up with rosettes of white satin ribbon. The bodice was trimmed with orange blossom, and the same flowers decorated a lace veil held in place by five diamond stars, the gift of the bridegroom. Mr McEwan gave his stepdaughter away, and Mrs McEwan wore a dress of sapphire velvet finely embroidered in a design of small pink roses. Across the aisle, Lady Greville, the mother of the groom, countered with a more sombre dress of dark olive-green velvet, and a bonnet appliquéd with shaded pansies. A detachment of fellow-officers from the groom's regiment, the 1st

Right: **Margaret Helen Anderson, painted by the society portraitist Hermann Schmiechen, in 1889, when she was 26 years old.**

Life Guards, lined the aisle of the church. The Revd J.W. Ayre led the choral service, but the choir was notably tuneless and ragged in performance.

The newly married couple and their guests returned to the McEwans' home, 4, Chesterfield Gardens, where Mrs McEwan stood at the top of the stairs to welcome them into a substantial wedding breakfast, consisting of every luxury, from plovers' eggs to asparagus, gargantuan strawberries, and a giant wedding cake.

There was also an astonishing cornucopia of wedding presents. Guards were placed in the drawing room to protect the 200 gifts, and visitors were particularly keen to get close to the spectacular jewellery. *The Scotsman* remarked (slightly ungrammatically) that the haul was '…perhaps the most valuable collection of wedding presents that any, not royal, bride has received these many long years.' The diamond tiara, made of the finest stones, was estimated to be worth £50,000; it was the gift of Mr McEwan to the bride, together with a beautiful diamond corsage in a design of leaves, while her mother gave her a gold-mounted travelling-bag. Lord Greville's present was a diamond and emerald bracelet, and Lady Greville gave an antique cross of turquoises and brilliants.

A massive silver bowl and candelabra was supplied by the workmen at McEwan's brewery, and the 1st Life Guards subscribed to a hammered silver bowl and an ostrich feather and tortoiseshell fan. There were also canteens of cutlery, clocks, walking sticks, exquisite dinner and dessert services. *The Worcester Herald* remarked, 'The marriage, which is prompted by affection on both sides, will enable Miss Anderson to claim kinship with many titled families…' That, of course, had always been the intention.

The celebrations were not confined to London; while the wedding party was under way in Mayfair, Mr McEwan had bankrolled a dinner for 468, the entire staff of Fountain Brewery, at the Music Hall in Edinburgh. Dinner was provided by the Head Chef of the Café Royal Hotel, and a band provided the music. Speech followed speech, with ever more extravagant hyperbole. Toast after toast was drunk with the greatest heartiness; it was obviously a night to remember.

Meanwhile, Ronald and Margaret left to spend the first week of their honeymoon at Oatlands Park Hotel, Surrey. Subsequently they travelled to Paris, and it was at this time that Mrs Greville was painted by Carolus-Duran (1837–1917), renowned for his racy, knowing portraits of ladies from French society. In painting Margaret Greville, he produced an unusual and striking full-length portrait of considerable *brio*, a foretaste of John Singer Sargent's later 'swagger' portraits (Carolus-Duran was Sargent's tutor). The new Mrs Greville is dressed in a well-cut but slightly austere outfit, a black dress with a white *fichu* neckline, without a single piece of jewellery, not even a wedding ring, perhaps surprising considering her passion for jewellery. What is convincing however is the vivacity of the figure and face; Margaret Greville was no longer the 'shrinking violet' depicted in the 1889 portrait by Schmiechen, she was now a cosmopolitan and polished woman of the world.

> *Margaret Greville was no longer the 'shrinking violet' depicted in the 1886 portrait by Schmiechen, she was now a cosmopolitan and polished woman of the world.*

On their return to London the Grevilles moved into Lord Cloncurry's house in Deanery Street, rented for them by Mr McEwan. Ronnie and Maggie, as they called each other, had survived the public ordeal of a fashionable wedding, and married life stretched out ahead of them. They were popular, lively and well-connected. Thanks to her stepfather, they could depend upon a five-figure annual income. They socialised with Ronnie's dearest friend George Keppel and his charming and popular wife, Alice, and were members of the informal court around the Prince of Wales, whose leisure activities included field sports, gambling and discreet philandering. Maggie engaged the services of a press clippings agency. Almost none of those cuttings pre-dates 1891; so far as she was concerned, those aspects of her life she was prepared to make public had begun only once she was the Honourable Mrs Greville, safe from speculation about her surname and origins. Becoming Mr McEwan's stepdaughter had been her first great leap; marriage to Ronnie was her second metamorphosis.

Society Launch

The Grevilles

Through marriage, the newly minted Margaret Greville found herself in a different world. Her congenial husband, the easy-going Ronnie, heir to a title and an impressive estate, also had a complex family. His mother, the formidable Lady Violet Greville, *née* Graham was the daughter of the 4th Duke of Montrose and a Scottish aristocrat. Lady Violet was a gifted writer and journalist whose features appeared in English-language papers all over the world. She wrote passionately and entertainingly on diverse subjects of the day, championing the cause of independence for women. Born in 1842, she married in 1863, and was a commanding presence until her death at the advanced age of 90. As an early proto-feminist, she must have been an unnerving mother-in-law, not least because she frequently declaimed in print the shortcomings of the modern woman.

In 1892, Lady Greville published *The Gentlewoman in Society*, a guide to contemporary etiquette, aimed at the newly rich. Her advice was worldly in tone; for example, dinner parties were not intended to be a pleasure, merely a reciprocal obligation, or 'cutlet for cutlet'. However, she was a sincere advocate of social freedom for women, encouraging independence, curiosity, education and travel. She also had a strong social conscience; in the autumn of 1888, using the public revulsion at the 'Jack the Ripper' murders in the East End of London, Lady Violet campaigned for funds to support a 'lying-in hospital' for destitute women in Shadwell, in an effort to improve women's lives in that benighted part of the capital.

While Lady Violet dominated her immediate family, her brother-in-law, Patrick Greville-Nugent, born in 1852, was the proverbial 'black sheep'. In 1892, a year after Margaret married Ronald, Uncle Patrick found himself in very hot water. He was 40 years old, a very prominent citizen, a Deputy Lieutenant and magistrate of County Westmeath in Ireland. Married with a daughter, he had a prestigious London home at Eaton Terrace. He was charged with indecently assaulting a Miss Marion Lymetta Price of Vauxhall, in a first-class carriage of the Brighton to London train on the night of 18 April. At the initial hearing, he denied everything, protesting vigorously that Miss Price was attempting to blackmail him. The case was referred for trial at the North London Sessions, while he was released on bail of £400.

Right: **Debutantes at Buckingham Palace after being presented to Queen Victoria, pictured in the *Illustrated London News*, 21 May 1892.**

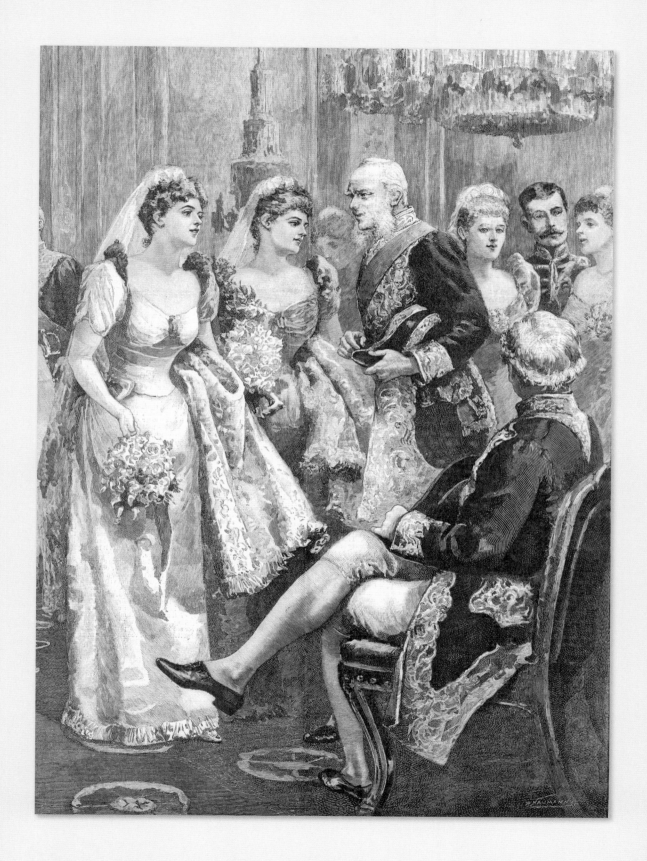

Sensationally, when the case came to court, he changed his plea and admitted the charge of common assault, though denying the more serious offence of indecent assault. He pleaded drunkenness in extenuation, and was sentenced to six months' imprisonment and hard labour. He was dismissed from the office of Deputy Lieutenant. The case was reported prominently in American and Australian papers, especially *The New York Times*, yet it did not appear at all in British newspapers; influence had been exerted to suppress the story.

In January 1891, Ronnie's father had been bitten by a mad dog. The dog was shot, and Lord Greville left immediately for the Pasteur Institute in Paris, taking with him the deceased retriever. The dog's remains were tested, and it had indeed contracted rabies. A bite from a rabid dog had always been a death sentence for humans, but the Pasteur Institute had recently developed an antidote, and Lord Greville underwent 21 inoculations. He survived to campaign for the creation of a Pasteur Institute in Britain, attributing his survival to their knowledge. Facing threats of rabies and sexual scandals, the origins of little Miss Anderson were the least of the Grevilles' concerns.

London life and presentation at Court

Margaret was introduced to Ronnie's well-heeled friends. She quickly became a close friend of Mrs Alice Keppel, a Scottish-born beauty whose father was the Conservative MP for Stirlingshire. Five years younger than Margaret, Alice married handsome George Keppel, third son of the 7th Earl of Albemarle, in June 1891, just two months after the Grevilles' wedding. Margaret, proud of her Scottish origins, enjoyed the company of her popular, pretty and socially confident friend.

However, to be part of the élite of London society, a young lady had to be 'presented at Court' to the monarch, a procedure that required sponsorship by a former debutante. Between 1880 and 1900, the number of presentations at Court virtually doubled, to accommodate the numbers of the marriageable daughters who lacked aristocratic origins or massive estates. The new Mrs Greville's background was a barrier to her presentation; it was more than a year after her marriage, in May 1892, that she made her debut at Buckingham Palace. Lady Greville, needless to say, was caustic about the practice:

"Now, there is no rule or reason for attendance at Court. Rich merchants; people in business; country squires; American cousins; people of no estimation except their own; people who are never under any possible circumstances likely to be invited to State balls or parties – all these crowd and press and gather together, and think their season in London utterly wasted unless they have made their bow to the Sovereign."

(The Gentlewoman in Society, *1892, p. 112*)

Nevertheless, schooled in the protocol, bearing a lengthy train, and with a headdress of three white ostrich feathers, the Honourable Mrs Ronnie Greville was presented by the Duchess of Montrose, her husband's aunt by marriage. Debutantes' families would crack open the safe and retrieve the best jewels they could muster for this occasion. Diamond tiaras were *de rigeur*; these would be borrowed, or even hired for the day, if the family could not provide a decent 'fender' of its own. Margaret Greville, with Mr McEwan's considerable fortune behind her, was sporting the beautiful diamond tiara her father had given her on her wedding day.

Ronnie's political career

Accustomed to her father's political influence, Margaret encouraged her husband to stand as an MP. His first attempt, in the General Election of 1895, was unsuccessful, but he had acquitted himself well, and the following year he was adopted as the Conservative candidate for East Bradford, in Yorkshire. Captain Greville still held a commission in the army. At a public meeting he was heckled for being a soldier and the son of a peer; he stated robustly that he was proud of the former, and couldn't help the latter, which won the audience to his side. *The Guardian* (9 November 1896) said that Ronnie '… knows very little of national affairs. His blunders are ludicrous, and of trade and labour questions he understands nothing; but he is modest, and on Saturday pleaded, "I am young, have plenty of energy, and am willing to learn." … they will vote on Tuesday for Captain Greville because his world is so very far removed from their own…'

Ronald won the seat by a narrow margin in November 1896, with support from his more experienced friend, Mr Winston Churchill, MP, who visited Bradford during the campaign. Before long it was evident that Ronald Greville was better at being a gentleman of leisure; he only spoke publicly in the House of Commons eleven times in a decade, usually only to ask questions. However, he did have a life beyond Parliament, as a Justice of the Peace and Deputy Lieutenant, as well as High Sheriff for County Westmeath in Ireland. He was a member of various clubs, including the Naval and Military, the Carlton and the Turf, and he spent a great deal of time following horse-racing, playing golf and socialising, often in attendance on the Prince of Wales.

Racing, Edward and Mrs Keppel

The racecourse was a melting-pot for late Victorian and Edwardian society at all levels. Fortunes were won and lost on the result of a race, and to be the owner of a race horse added extra excitement to every race-meeting. Much of Margaret and Ronald's new married life revolved around race-meetings; the Grevilles, with their friends the Keppels and the Saviles, would spend days attending races, thrilled by the excitement of the crowds and mingling with high society.

Below: **The Hon. Mrs George Keppel and her elder daughter, Violet, in 1899.**

For fashionable society ladies, race-going was demanding. Consuelo Vanderbilt, a friend of Margaret's, was an American heiress who was unhappily married to the Duke of Marlborough. They would rent a house for Ascot Week and invite many of their friends to stay or to dine. She spent afternoons in lavish outfits meeting acquaintances in the Royal Enclosure. Enormous sums were spent on costumes, especially for Gold Cup Day on the Thursday. Central to their social life was the future Edward VII, another great enthusiast of the 'sport of kings'. He first encountered Mrs Alice Keppel, who was to become his last and best-loved mistress, at Sandown Races in 1898, when he was 58 and she was 29. Shortly afterwards, the Prince dined with Alice Keppel and her husband George in their house in Belgravia. In the words of Sir Philip Magnus, 'an understanding arose overnight…'

Once the relationship was established, the Keppels accompanied Edward to many of his social engagements, and frequently joined him on his travels. The Keppels thus introduced the Grevilles into the most intimate royal circles, staying at country houses as part of Edward's retinue. The newspapers of the era blandly list the social whirl around the Royal Family and mention the Keppels, the Grevilles and the King with due deference. Typical is the account in the *Observer* of 19 May 1907, reporting on the previous week's racing: 'At Newmarket there was a larger attendance than any day of the week, and the King was, of course, an early arrival on the scene. Mrs George Keppel was chatting for a long time with Mrs Ronald Greville…'

The Keppels thus introduced the Grevilles into the most intimate royal circles, staying at country houses as part of Edward's retinue.

George Keppel's complicity in his wife's infidelity might seem odd, but he was aware of her previous dalliances with well-off men, and he believed that she would always come back to him in the end. They were extremely fond of each other, and when in 1901 George contracted typhoid in New York, Alice and her brother-in-law, the Earl of Albemarle, raced across the Atlantic to take care of him. Interestingly, Queen Alexandra wrote her a letter expressing genuine sympathy for her 'great anxiety'; the Queen tolerated Mrs Keppel's role in the life of her spectacularly unfaithful husband. Alice's tact and discretion was an improvement on the high-handed behaviour of some of his previous mistresses.

So close were the Grevilles and the Keppels that Margaret was godmother to their second daughter, Sonia, a relationship Maggie treasured. When Sonia was born, in 1900, Alice was known to be the lover of the King, but she insisted that her husband, George, was Sonia's father, which caused a *frisson* in their circle of intimates. It had been assumed, wrongly, that George had relinquished the marital bed in deference to his monarch. This gave the Prince of Wales pause for thought, but made Alice even more desirable in his eyes. Mindful of the sensitivities regarding the baby's parentage, childless Margaret Greville offered to adopt her, but was politely rebuffed; Sonia was the Keppels' daughter, and would be brought up in the Keppel household, with her older sister, Violet.

Subsequently, Sonia remembered the heady social whirl at her parents' house; there was 'Kingy', with his beard, cigars and plummy voice; Sir Ernest Cassel, the financier, who bore a striking resemblance to his monarch, which occasionally confused her; Sir Thomas Lipton, who had made a fortune in the grocery trade; Lady Sarah Wilson, the heroine of the Siege of Ladysmith; and her godmother, Mrs Greville, who provided her with fabulous presents.

Alice Keppel's exemplary behaviour was such that she and the understanding George were even invited to stay at Sandringham by Queen Alexandra. On one occasion, the Queen spotted her extremely portly husband and the bosomy Mrs Keppel wedged together into an open carriage. The sight of the two well-upholstered lovers suddenly struck her as comical, and she burst into laughter.

On one occasion, the Queen spotted her extremely portly husband and the bosomy Mrs Keppel wedged into an open carriage.

The reason for Edward's endless pursuit of pleasure was because his apprenticeship as heir to the throne was otherwise lengthy and tedious; his reclusive mother, Victoria, grimly refused to share with her son the duties she fulfilled through her endless 'red boxes'. However, she mellowed sufficiently to co-operate in the celebrations of her six decades' tenure on the throne. In 1897, the nation threw itself into marking the Diamond Jubilee, and all were swept up in a mood of royalistic euphoria.

Even the Empress Queen could not live forever and the longest reign in British history ended on 22 January 1901. Queen Victoria died at the age of 81, surrounded by her family: the Prince and Princess of Wales, their son the Duke of York, who was to become King George V, three of the Queen's daughters, and the monarch's rather pushy grandson, Kaiser Wilhelm II of Germany, known as 'Cousin Willy', who had turned up on his own initiative.

Victoria had been declining in health for over a year, but her demise still came as a shock. Her withdrawal from public life to mourn Albert had caused much resentment during her lifetime, but some wondered openly about the suitability of the new king. The American-born novelist Henry James remarked: 'We feel motherless today. We are to have no more of little mysterious Victoria, but instead fat, vulgar, dreadful Edward.' Now nearly 60, Edward was a burly, bearded playboy, and was well-known on the

Continent for his high-spending, pleasure-loving excursions, accompanied by a well-heeled entourage. Easily bored, he had expended his considerable energies and fortune pursuing personal pleasures. *The Times* leader, on the first day of his reign, remarked gloomily, 'We shall not pretend that there is nothing in his long career which those who respect and admire him would not wish otherwise.'

Edward began by tackling the renovation of the royal palaces, which under Victoria had become dusty memorials to the memory of Albert, dead for four decades. Having referred to Buckingham Palace as 'the Mausoleum', he ordered that the sanitation, heating and lighting of the royal residences be upgraded. Edward had a good eye, and he scoured the royal collections for neglected fine furniture and magnificent paintings, which were used to adorn the newly decorated, brilliantly lit rooms of the royal palaces.

Above: **Alice Keppel, 'La Favorita' of Edward VII, in a portrait miniature painted by Gertrude Massey, c.1903.**

The Coronation

The Coronation was finally held on 9 August 1902 in Westminster Abbey, a lengthy event which tested the nerves and stamina of all involved. Peers and peeresses filled the rows of seats. In the chancel sat the royal princesses and above them was a rank of seating quickly dubbed the King's 'Loose Box'. It was the place where the new monarch wanted all his favourite lady friends to sit; there was Alice Keppel and her mother-in-law, Lady Albemarle; Alice's best friend, Mrs Ronnie Greville; Lady Sarah Wilson; Mrs Arthur Paget; the actress Sarah Bernhardt; the king's former mistresses Daisy Warwick and Lillie Langtry; Jennie Churchill, mother of Winston, her sister Leonie Jerome and Princess Daisy of Pless. It was apparent to all that these ladies were trusted intimates of the King, for a variety of reasons.

Following the Coronation, the new monarchs quickly established a new style at court; under the old Queen, formal occasions had been solemn and largely silent, with only the monarch allowed to initiate a conversation. By contrast, the new royals were jolly and chatty; Queen Alexandra found these receptions rather a trial as she was becoming increasingly deaf, but she coped by smiling and nodding at whatever she was told. Sociable and jocular Edward, at last relieved of the basilisk stare of maternal disapproval, threw himself into the fray, surrounded by his closest and most trusted friends.

Edwardian Hostess

"[It] would be punishment indeed for some of us suddenly to find ourselves transformed into very rich, very smart, very ambitious Edwardian hostesses."

(*J.B. Priestley,* The Edwardians)

Inheriting the throne did not deter Edward from the pursuit of pleasure. He continued to attend race-meetings, to spend long weekends at the country houses of his friends (accompanied sometimes by his wife) and to go about with beautiful women. Some criticised his conduct, calling him 'Edward the Caresser', but there were many who rejoiced that the monarch should share their own diversions. He was, in the pithy phrase of J.B. Priestley, '…a typical Englishman *with the lid off.*'

Biarritz was Edward's favourite French resort; he paid five-week visits to the French Riviera, setting out around the middle of March and breaking his journey in Paris at either end of the holiday. Although he was supposedly travelling *en garçon*, he was accompanied by a select band of his closest friends. The group usually included the Marquis Luis de Soveral, known as the 'Blue Monkey' because of his swarthy complexion. The Marquis was Portuguese Ambassador to London; he and the King had been friends since the 1870s when they had explored the racier side of Berlin's nightlife. Another valued friend was Consuelo, Duchess of Manchester, who rented a villa every year at Biarritz around Easter to entertain King Edward and his entourage. But the focus of his attention was 'Little Mrs George', Alice Keppel, who for the last four years

of the King's life (1906–10), would join him in Biarritz for at least three weeks in early spring, taking her children, as well as a retinue of staff. As soon as she set foot on French soil she was treated with the gallantry and deference the French felt due to the Royal Mistress, unlike in London society.

Sir Ernest Cassel, Edward VII's financial advisor, rented the Villa Eugenie at Biarritz, a house that had once belonged to the Empress Josephine. Mrs Keppel and her family would stay as guests of the Cassels, while the King occupied a special suite at the Hotel du Palais. Mrs Keppel flitted between the two residences.

At Biarritz, the royal retinue would spend their time motoring to beauty spots, attending displays of flying machines and watching pelota games. On Easter Sunday a fleet of motorcars would set out for a massive picnic, an event His Majesty liked to think was entirely impromptu, but had been planned like a military campaign by his staff. He had a habit of consuming seven-course picnics on grassy roadside banks, a practice that inevitably attracted a crowd.

Right: **King Edward VII in 1907, known to some of his subjects as 'Edward the Caresser'.**

On 14 March 1909 the *Observer* ran a studiedly innocent report of the King's holiday at Biarritz, reporting on the poor weather and His Majesty's excursions on the sea front, golf courses and by motorcar. They mentioned that Consuelo, Duchess of Manchester, was already there, along with Ernest Cassel, who was hosting Lord and Lady Savile. Mrs Ronald Greville was due imminently, but of 'La Favorita' there was no mention. Discretion was all in royal circles.

Mrs Greville enjoyed gossip, but avoided naming its subject if the story was damaging. Monte Carlo provided discreet sensual pleasures for the wealthy and she recalled a tale of a famous Russian beauty who went to live there in 1892, with the Grand Duke X. While her protector was absent, she was visited by his cousin, the Grand Duke Y. Eight years later Mrs Greville was staying at the resort with Mr McEwan, who was being treated by a famous Swiss doctor. Entering the hotel lift one evening, she was asked by the Grand Duke X if their doctor was skilful, as his young son had TB. Mrs Greville was surprised; she had never heard of the boy but heartily recommended the doctor. Six months later she returned to Monte Carlo, and the doctor asked her advice. He had successfully treated the young boy and had received a cheque for 3,000 francs and a letter of thanks for saving the life of his son, signed by the Grand Duke X. However, shortly after, he had also received a similarly effusive letter and a cheque for the same amount, signed by Grand Duke Y – what should he do? 'Accept both cheques,' Mrs Greville replied firmly. 'Never impugn a woman's honour!'

Such double standards applied in the Grevilles' social circles, particularly the opportunities offered for adultery by country house weekends. Many married couples in the higher echelons had chosen their spouses from a limited pool of suitable candidates. They married for social or financial advancement, and, as long as the parentage of the 'heir and the spare' was beyond reproach, some latitude was often allowed. Divorce was a great scandal to be avoided at all costs. Affairs of the heart, if they were discreet, were largely tolerated and even condoned by broad-minded hostesses, such as Mrs Ronnie Greville. 'I don't follow people into their bedrooms', she said. 'It's what they do outside them that's important.'

Royal house parties

Edward VII was keen to keep his social circle close, taking every opportunity to enjoy himself whenever the occasion arose. In September 1903, for example, the King stayed at Rufford Hall in Nottinghamshire as the guest of the Saviles for Doncaster Race Week. The Saviles were near neighbours and close friends of the Grevilles in Charles Street, Mayfair; because of their friendship with the King, the couples were known in some quarters as 'the Civils and the Grovels'. Travelling on the same train were the Honourable Ronald and Mrs Greville, Consuelo, the Dowager Duchess of Manchester, the Marquis de Soveral, and Mrs George Keppel, noticeably without her husband.

The King's mobile court accompanied him to Alice Keppel's childhood home, Duntreath Castle, in September 1909, as guests of her parents, Sir Archibald and Lady Edmonstone. Mrs Greville, Lady Sarah Wilson and the Keppels travelled on the royal train with the King. They arrived at Blanesfield Station, which had been lavishly decorated with flowers, and the next day more than 5,000 people turned out to watch the King and his party attend the local church at Strathblane. The party took tea at Buchanan Castle with the Duke and Duchess of Montrose; Mrs Greville had a family connection, as her mother-in-law had been a daughter of the family.

The King particularly enjoyed the company of his closest friends at intimate little dinners in London. In December 1903, the Grevilles entertained King Edward for dinner at their house at 11, Charles Street. By now Ronald and Margaret Greville had made many new friends. For three successive Christmases, 1901, 1902 and 1903, they were among the house party of about 30 guests hosted by the Duke and Duchess of Devonshire at Chatsworth.

Mrs Greville was also an early adopter of the practice of 'dining out' in hotel restaurants, a comparatively new idea for ladies in British society. Living close to the newly built Ritz hotel and more venerable Claridge's, Mrs Greville patronised their restaurants, along with a plethora of society names such as Lady Cunard; the two socialites were to become great rivals for more than three decades.

London was the hub of the social scene, and the Grevilles went to considerable trouble and expense to provide a suitably opulent setting at their home in Charles Street, Mayfair. However, in order to return the hospitality of their aristocratic circle, they also needed a country place where they could entertain in some style. It was only a matter of time before Mr McEwan's vast fortune was employed to expand further the Grevilles' horizons, this time into the lush and leafy Home Counties.

Polesden Lacey and Widowhood

"A peep of beautiful distance."　　　　(*Joseph Farington, 1803*)

The expansion of the railways and the coming of the motorcar made country house weekends appealing to the wealthy, especially if a place could be found not far from London. The Grevilles started to look for a suitable 'country seat' to buy. From 1902 they occasionally rented Reigate Priory, an attractive place, which was effectively a holiday cottage for the élite.

In May 1905 Margaret and Ronald hosted a house party at Reigate Priory for Edward VII, inviting the Duke and Duchess of Devonshire, the Prime Minister, Arthur Balfour, Ernest Cassel, the Cadogans, Lord and Lady Savile, Mr McEwan and Alice Keppel. A photograph of the guests shows the hostess, Mrs Greville, sitting at the King's right, far closer to him than Alice Keppel; Mr McEwan and Ronald Greville stand in the back row, with Ronnie clutching a dog. As Sonia Keppel was to remark of her godmother, 'Throughout most of Kingy's reign, I can see her, small but forceful, making her way to the front of any company she was in.'

Polesden Lacey

In 1906 Polesden Lacey was on the market, following the death of Sir Clinton Edward

Dawkins. Close to Great Bookham in Surrey, this was a substantial house on a hillside looking over a wooded valley, with spectacular views. The estate encompassed two farms and a great deal of agricultural land. The house had been designed by Thomas Cubitt from 1819–21, and then almost entirely rebuilt by Dawkins' architect, Ambrose Poynter, with the installation of electricity and central heating. Mrs Greville was given £80,000 by her father to buy the estate (approximately £4.5 million today), and the couple commissioned an ambitious programme of refurbishment, to transform the house over a period of two years. Meanwhile, they continued to entertain in London, with occasional trips to Reigate Priory, a perfect base from which to supervise the work. In May 1907 the King spent Whitsun at the Priory with the Grevilles. So advanced were the improvements that when Mrs Greville motored over to inspect progress on the property, her car was not able to reach the house because the drive had been dug up.

The redesign of Polesden Lacey was the work of architects Mewès and Davis, fresh from their triumph on the London Ritz hotel. Charles Mewès was born in Alsace and had Baltic Jewish origins; his much younger, English partner, Arthur J. Davis, was the son of a Jewish

Left: **The east front of Polesden Lacey in the snow.**

businessman. They specialised in creating modern buildings in traditional French style, fitted with the very latest engineering and technological innovations. They used a steel frame, for example, for the London Ritz, so that the building could rise many storeys, yet the arcade at street level recalls the rue de Rivoli in Paris. The Ritz interior is ornate and French in style, known jocularly as 'tous les Louis', with much use of *trompe l'oeil*, mirrors and gilding to overcome the narrowness of the site. Lush and sophisticated, the Ritz was the reinforced concrete embodiment of the expansionist Edwardian spirit; it expressed *entente cordiale*, the 'special relationship' between French and British culture. Mewès and Davis became a byword among the well-travelled rich, and it is typical of Mrs Greville's ability for talent-spotting that she employed the most successful hotel designers available to create a country house dedicated to leisure and pleasure.

The redesign of Polesden Lacey was the work of architects Mewès and Davis, fresh from their triumph on the London Ritz hotel.

Polesden Lacey is built as an open square, around a central courtyard, onto which French windows open to allow extra light. The long corridors are lined with wood panelling, and the floors covered with plain red runners. Three of these corridors housed much of Mrs Greville's eclectic collection of paintings and *objets d'art*, from important Dutch old masters to rare Chinese export ware ceramics, and a Roman sarcophagus. The ceiling of the corridor is curved and covered with intricate moulded plaster, similar to the Jacobean ceiling at Chastleton House in Oxfordshire.

Mrs Greville's architects extended the south side of the house to match the kitchen wing, and both were fitted with bow windows, although the kitchen windows were 'blind'. Above, at first floor level, was Mrs Greville's self-contained apartment, with adjacent bedrooms for her personal maid, a sitting room and luxurious bathrooms. Mrs Greville's bedroom contained lacquered furniture and an ornate bed in the Chinese Chippendale style. The refurbished house had eighteen bedrooms, eleven *en suite* bathrooms, electricity, central heating, and ample hot water.

On the ground floor of the south side of the house is a sequence of ornate reception rooms; Mrs Greville had instructed her architects, 'I want a room I can entertain Maharajahs in…', and they were as good as their word.

Left: **The Saloon at Polesden Lacey, extravagantly carved and panelled.**

The huge Saloon, which was a riot of red brocade and gilded *boiseries* salvaged from an eighteenth-century Italian palazzo, was flanked on one side by Mrs Greville's study and library, and on the other by a tearoom of exquisite decoration.

The Bachelor Wing was extremely masculine in style, recalling a gentleman's club of the turn of the century, with a billiard table, writing desks and groups of back-buttoned leather armchairs. A product of the Victorian age, Mrs Greville was aware that gentlemen liked to be able to escape female company occasionally, so she also provided a smoking room. Next door is a gunroom, and a side door leads to the grounds, so that men going on a shoot could leave the house early, and dispose of wet or muddy footwear for their valets to tackle on their return.

In redesigning Polesden Lacey, Margaret and Ronnie Greville had created a setting fit for a king, a sanctuary where the monarch could feel comfortable with friends and safe from censure. As Edward was to be their most important house guest, a great deal of thought went into the design of his private suite. Facing south, it consisted of a bedroom, a sitting room and a bathroom, opening off an inner lobby, like the best suites at the Ritz. The bedroom was furnished throughout with Louis XVI furniture upholstered in pale blue-green silk, the walls were panelled in white and the carpet was pale grey. There was a marquetry writing table placed in front of one of the windows. The double bed had a carved and gilded bedhead and rose brocade hangings, with a tall gilded candelabra on either side of the mirror. The adjoining sitting room contained magnificent lacquered furniture. The *en suite* bathroom had a white marble floor, with walls of unpolished marble, while all the fittings, except the marble washstand supported on silver legs, were of plate glass. It was the last word in luxury.

Bereavement and widowhood

But while Polesden Lacey was being transformed into the very
best sort of hotel, Margaret lost two of the people most dear
to her. While the first half of 1906 was full of social events
with the King and his circle, the autumn and winter were
overshadowed by the death of Helen McEwan, Margaret's
mother, at the age of 70. She died on 3 September 1906 at
16, Charles Street, of 'acute nephritis, exhaustion and general
dropsy'. In Helen's will, made in 1903, she left all her personal
belongings to her daughter. She left shares to Ronnie and her
godson, and £500 each to her three closest female friends, a
countess and the wives of two MPs. The remainder was split
equally between bequests to the Royal Hospital, Chelsea, and
the Gordon Boys Home in London. Interestingly, she appears
to have left nothing to her family, the Andersons, from an estate
with a gross value of £20,749, a substantial sum for a woman
who had been a lodging house-keeper two decades before. Mrs
McEwan was buried at Highgate Cemetery, and sincerely
mourned by both her husband and her daughter, who now
invited the elderly widower to stay as often as possible.

Above: **A miniature portrait of Ronald
Greville, 1864–1908.**

Worse was to come. Margaret and Ronald had enjoyed planning the
changes at Polesden Lacey. In 1906 affable Ronnie, at the age of 42,
resigned from politics. He had never been a committed MP, and he now
wanted to divide his time between their home in central London, the estate
in Surrey and socialising with the King's circle. He was looking forward to
participating in more equestrian sports, as there were excellent rides and
impressive stables at Polesden. In addition, Ronnie also enjoyed motoring,
buying first a 12hp steam Serpolet in 1901, then a Panhard, employing two
chauffeurs and a 'washer' to care for them. Ronnie had drawn up ambitious
and intricate plans for terracing and planting the south-facing garden and,
had it not been for their apparent inability to have children, their marriage
seems to have been blessed by great good fortune as well as a genuine love
for each other.

A keen race-goer and a life-long cigar-smoker, Ronnie was at Aintree
Racecourse at the end of March 1908 when he became ill, and returned

to London to his doctors. The news was grave; he had cancer of the vocal
chords, and he was operated on to remove the larynx without delay.
The newspapers were persuaded to print only positive bulletins about
his condition, as Maggie did not want 'some penny-a-line to publish
"malignant" and eliminate all hope from my beloved one'. Ronnie survived
the two-hour operation, but he subsequently contracted pneumonia, dying
within a week on Sunday 5 April 1908, aged only 43, at their home in
11, Charles Street.

The Grevilles' friends were shocked by the rapidity of his
death. Letters and telegrams of condolence poured in;
Janet Younger, Mr McEwan's sister, wrote: 'So grieved at
the sad news. Deepest sympathy in your great loss. May
you be strengthened to bear it bravely.' Others spoke of
Ronnie's kindness to them, and it is apparent that he was
genuinely popular and well-liked. From Osterley Park,
Lord Villiers wrote: '...when one thinks how much one will
miss him as a personal friend, I can the more realize what
his loss must mean to you, especially having spent so many pleasant
Sundays with you both at Reigate [Priory] and seen what a happy home
you had. I can only hope that it may be of some consolation to you to
know, as of course you do know, how genuinely his loss is lamented by all
who knew him...'

> *'So grieved at the sad
> news. Deepest sympathy
> in your great loss. May
> you be strengthened to
> bear it bravely.'*

Ronnie was buried on 9 April 1908, in Great Bookham Churchyard.
The grave had been lined with white lilies and azaleas by Mr Lane, Head
Gardener at Polesden Lacey. The principal mourners were the widow and
Lord and Lady Greville. Major Holford, who had been the couple's best
man, now had the melancholy task of representing the King. Also present
were the Duke of Montrose (Ronnie's uncle), George Keppel, Lord Herbert
Vane-Tempest (later Lord Londonderry), Lord Ilchester, Mr McEwan's
nephews, the household servants and estate employees led by Mr Bole,
Head Steward, and Mr Mahony, Ronnie's Irish valet.

George Keppel sent a wreath bearing the message 'In memory of my oldest
and best friend'. A beautiful wreath of lilies of the valley and arum lilies was
simply inscribed 'From the King'. At the other end of the social spectrum,
Freda Smith, whose mother was the Polesden gardeners' cook, remembered

attending the funeral at the age of eight with the other schoolchildren. She recalled it as a very solemn 'horse and carriage affair', with the children wearing their best clothes.

It is apparent that Margaret sincerely mourned Ronnie. Her young groom Arthur Thompson remarked how 'the spark went out of her' after Ronnie's death. For the first year she barely went out in society, in keeping with the rituals expected of her. Her elderly father was a source of comfort. However, she was not forgotten by her old friends; even while still in mourning, she was encouraged by the King's circle to socialise, on the subdued level appropriate to her status as a widow. Gradually she started seeing people again in a quiet way. She also had companionship from a number of pet dogs: five Pekingese and a white collie.

Because of Ronnie's death, the King's planned inaugural visit to Polesden Lacey was postponed for a year, until 5 and 6 June 1909, when the group assembled to entertain him was select but perfectly chosen. This was to be almost her first social engagement since Ronnie's death; the very first had been a 'dry run' weekend at the end of May 1909, hosting old friends, to make sure that everything ran smoothly.

A beautiful wreath of lilies of the valley and arum lilies was simply inscribed 'From the King'.

Entertaining Edward

Having the King to stay was an ordeal for any hostess. Edward liked at least 20 guests, but no more than 40; the majority should already be his friends, and if there were newcomers, he preferred the illusion that everyone knew each other. The part of the house where he was staying should be a self-contained suite, with Mrs Keppel's room nearby, if she was one of the guests. A telegraph room was also required, so that the King could be in constant contact with his government.

The King could also be a martyr to boredom. Wise hostesses recognised the warning signs: his eyelids blinking more slowly than usual, his voice slowing, his fingers drumming impatiently on the table. He would often sit in silence at a meal, fiddling with the cutlery, which unnerved those unused to him. His apparent *ennui* was because he wearied of acting as the 'ringmaster' at

Left: Edward VII at Polesden Lacey in 1909. Mrs Greville is seated on his right; Mrs Keppel is second on his left.

social events. Indeed, he preferred general conversation, listening to others' views and forming his own conclusions. Mrs Greville understood him, and made a point of providing intelligent company, constant stimulus and the unobtrusive luxury that Edward most appreciated.

The King's visit to Polesden Lacey

"The King left London yesterday afternoon on a visit to the Hon. Mrs Ronald Greville and her father, the Right Hon. William McEwan, at Polesden Lacey, when a small party of his intimate friends were invited to meet him."

(Observer, *6 June 1909*)

A great deal of effort – and money – had been expended to make Polesden Lacey as luxurious and as welcoming as possible for the visit of Edward VII. This royal weekend was a signal that not only was Margaret Greville returning to social life, but also that her country home was 'fit for a king' – it was a reassertion of her position as a valued intimate of royalty. The guest list had been approved in advance by the King, and it included most of his favourite people.

> *A great deal of effort – and money – had been expended to make Polesden Lacey as luxurious and as welcoming as possible for the visit of Edward VII.*

Supporting his daughter, Mr William McEwan was well respected by the monarch and had been appointed Privy Counsellor by him. Loyal friends Mr and Mrs George Keppel came with their daughter Sonia. Georgina, Countess of Dudley was an old flame of Edward's, and she brought her son, Mr John Ward. The intrepid Lady Sarah Wilson, who was the first woman war correspondent, was the

youngest daughter of the 7th Duke of Marlborough and aunt to Winston Churchill. Lady Sarah's nephew and his wife, Lord and Lady Alastair Innes-Ker, came too.

Other guests were the Marquis de Soveral, Portuguese Ambassador from 1884–1910, and a consummate Lothario; Count Albert Mensdorff, second cousin of Edward, who was Austrian Ambassador from 1904 till the Great War; and Sir John Willoughby, who had successfully served in the Boer War, survived imprisonment and had been involved in the Relief of Mafeking. Lady Violet Savile was one of Maggie's great friends; she and her husband were close neighbours, living at 12, Charles Street. Lady Violet was instrumental in encouraging Margaret back into public life, having her to stay, along with the King, at Rufford Abbey in September of the same year.

Edward VII also enjoyed the company of wealthy American ladies; Mrs George Cavendish-Bentinck was the daughter of Maturin Livingstone of

New York, and a member of Edward's inner circle. With such a group of intimates around him, the King was bound to enjoy his visit; indeed, he commended Mrs Greville, saying she had a 'positive genius for hospitality'. No detail escaped her attention; ample flowers filled every room and the latest novels would be left on every guest's bedside table. She employed excellent staff, and provided the very best food and wine.

Feeding the house party

In Edwardian high society the over-provision of ample food was like the constant grazing available on modern-day cruise liners. However, the intention was to offer a cornucopia of plenty, rather than an invitation to gluttony; it was understood that the diners would not eat everything, and canny hostesses such as Mrs Greville provided hand-written menus listing the numerous courses so that guests could 'pace' themselves.

Nevertheless, the ritual of meals gave a structure to the day; Polesden Lacey house guests would be brought tea in bed by a fleet of housemaids, with a few biscuits to give them the strength to rise and face the world. Breakfast was typically served between 8 and 10.30, a leisurely browse among the hot dishes of eggs, bacon, ham, sausage, kidneys, haddock and cold meats. For the more abstemious there was always porridge.

Lunch would be at 1.30; it might be *al fresco*, with the ladies joining the gentlemen if they were shooting. An elaborate picnic would be created by the chef, Mr Delachaume, and the servants, taking a laden pony and trap to carry all their equipment, would set up long tables and chairs in some idyllic spot on the estate, with napery, polished silver and glassware, to accommodate a group of 30 and their 8-course lunch of pies and ptarmigan. Afternoon tea consisted of delicious home-made cakes, exquisite sandwiches, and for King Edward, his favourite snack, lobster salad.

Dinner was at 8; usually a dozen courses, each small but delicious, and the finest of wines. Mrs Greville prided herself on her excellent cuisine and spared no expense. After dinner, the ladies would withdraw while the gentlemen passed round the port; when they rejoined the fairer sex, the indefatigable kitchen staff would lay out a buffet supper of sandwiches and cold meats, in case anyone still felt peckish.

Activities provided to entertain the house guests included golf, walking on the estate, riding or touring in motorcars, shooting in season, playing bridge or billiards, gossip and flirtation. It was a paradise for guests, with ample opportunities for leisure and pleasure, and a certain amount of latitude.

It was a paradise for guests, with ample opportunities for leisure and pleasure, and a certain amount of latitude.

Edward's inaugural visit to Polesden was a great success; with its landscaped grounds, attractive walks and individual walled gardens it provided a private, peaceful haven. The King instructed the Postmaster-General to arrange that the postman arriving at Polesden every morning should wait for an hour in the butler's pantry so that Mrs Greville could reply to any urgent letters that he would take on his departure; a considerable privilege that was still enjoyed by the household in the 1930s.

Return to Society

"The Hon. Mrs Ronald Greville, also a guest to meet the king, was in black. She is beginning to go out again now, and her presence is eagerly welcomed everywhere, for she is very kind, and nice, and sincere, things more appreciated in much-abused Society than you might think…"

(Lady's Pictorial, *18 September 1909*)

The visit of Edward VII to Polesden Lacey marked Margaret's return to social life, more than a year after Ronnie's death. However, there were many poignant reminders of her loss. Ronnie's younger brother, the Hon. Charles Beresford Fulke Greville, was now his father's heir. Probably in order to avoid having to attend Charles's London wedding, in mid-November 1909 Margaret went to New York, in the company of her friend the Hon. Lady Johnstone. Charles was marrying the beautiful Olive Grace Kerr, the widow of Henry S. Kerr, an American millionaire, on 15 November. While the ceremony took place in London with a reception at 22, Carlton House Terrace, Margaret Greville resolutely attended the Metropolitan Opera and caught up with her many East Coast friends.

While Charles and Olive were still on honeymoon, Lord Algernon Greville, Ronnie's father, died unexpectedly. Just two days after the wedding, at which he had appeared in excellent health and spirits, he had undergone a throat operation, and he did not survive, a melancholy echo of Ronnie's demise. The newlyweds abandoned their honeymoon and returned to London, and Margaret Greville returned to stay with her father at Charles Street. The funeral took place on 6 December 1909. Charles and Olive became the third Lord and Lady Greville, the title Ronald and Margaret would have inherited if he had lived a further eighteen months.

In the New Year of 1910 Margaret started to entertain at 11, Charles Street again, giving a small, smart dinner party every week. Significantly, she informed the newspapers about these events, to let society know that she was back in circulation. Diamonds and pearls were much favoured by Mrs Greville at this stage of her life; both had been established as appropriate gems for ladies in mourning by Queen Victoria, the recognised authority on the subject. By 1910, Mrs Greville had acquired a fine set of black diamonds, probably from Borneo. She was also buying decorative objects of great luxury; in March 1909 she had acquired a red and green gold lady's cigarette case made by Fabergé, with a diamond-encrusted pushpiece, which she had bought in the London branch. Smoking had become a fashionable habit among London society ladies and one needed a cigarette case of one's own, as well as a cigarette holder.

In March 1910 Margaret attended a big dinner party given by Lord and Lady Savile at their Charles Street home, in honour of the King, who was shortly to leave for his annual Biarritz holiday. Mrs Keppel, who would meet the monarch discreetly at the resort, wore a gown of oyster satin, caught up on one side by a huge diamond brooch. Mrs Greville was still in black, with a wide bandeau of diamonds in her hair.

Mrs Greville was still in black, with a wide bandeau of diamonds in her hair.

This was almost certainly the last time Margaret saw Edward VII alive. The King was now 68 years old and his general health was poor; although he was only 5 feet 7 inches tall, he weighed 16 stone and had a waist measurement of 48 inches. His appetite was voracious – he ate five meals a day – and he smoked twelve large cigars and at least twenty cigarettes a day. Mrs Keppel had long worried about his health; a damaged knee meant he took almost no exercise, and it was evident that he was not well.

'The King is dead…'

Shortly after his return from Biarritz, the King was diagnosed with severe bronchitis at Buckingham Palace on Monday 2 May 1910. Queen Alexandra was summoned from the Continent and she arrived on 5 May; the following day, the King saw his old friend Sir George Cassel to say goodbye.

There are differing accounts of Alice Keppel at the death-bed of Edward VII. She claimed later that Queen Alexandra had invited her to say farewell, but she became hysterical at the prospect of the King's death, creating what Viscount Esher described as 'a painful and rather theatrical exhibition'. Edward was treated with morphia, dying surrounded by his family at 11.45pm. Queen Alexandra wrote: 'He was the whole of my life, and now he is dead, nothing matters.' Those who had known the King were genuinely grief-stricken.

Edward's body lay in state for three days in Westminster Hall, and more than 250,000 people filed past the coffin to pay their respects. The funeral was held at Windsor on 20 May; the cortège was followed by eight kings and an emperor. Mrs Keppel attended the funeral in deepest mourning,

Below: **The pet cemetery at Polesden Lacey, with the grave of Edward VII's Airedale, Caesar, in the centre.**

but it was the silent sorrow of Queen Alexandra, who fell to her knees and covered her face with both hands as the coffin was lowered into the ground inside St George's Chapel that was most affecting.

Life goes on

There was a period of official mourning, but the new King and Queen announced that Royal Ascot would not be cancelled. What became known as 'Black Ascot' was a fitting tribute to the pleasure-loving monarch who had died only six weeks before. The sartorial rules for full mourning were obeyed; ladies were in deepest black and the gentlemen wore crepe bands on their hats. The race-cards had black borders, and the Royal Stand was closed, with the blinds of the Royal Box drawn. Meanwhile, Mrs Keppel, whose prostration had caused great concern to her friends and relations, had eventually rallied, and departed with her family on a trip to the Far East.

What became known as 'Black Ascot' was a fitting tribute to the pleasure-loving monarch who had died only six weeks before.

In November 1910 Mrs Greville commissioned a tiny Fabergé hardstone sculpture of Edward VII's favourite terrier, Caesar, and presented it to Queen Alexandra, as a memento. The Queen was very touched by this gesture, and Caesar was given to Mrs Greville, to live at Polesden Lacey, and was eventually buried in the pet cemetery. Meanwhile, the observant Sonia Keppel recalled how Margaret Greville was keen to cultivate Edward's successors, his son and daughter-in-law:

"...then Kingy himself died, but this interval of her mourning was shorter. Soon she was back near the throne of the new King and Queen, a person to be reckoned with and courted in any strata of society..."

The death of the King marked the end of a slightly louche episode encapsulated by Edward's brief reign. The new monarch, King George V, could not have been less like his father. He was peppery, unimaginative, uxorious, and devoted to duty and protocol. His idea of a perfect day involved wearing military uniforms, shooting birds, followed by a quiet evening at Sandringham with his stamp collection or writing up his game books. Queen Mary might knit a sock and smoke a cigarette. It was all very different from the nocturnal pleasures of 'Edward the Caresser'.

The New King and Queen and the First World War

"Dear Queen Mary, always so welcome, but never any notice!"

(*Margaret Greville quoted by Beverley Nichols in* The Sweet and Twenties)

Mrs Ronnie had become friendly with Edward VII's daughter-in-law, the former Princess Victoria Mary of Teck, who was known to her family as 'May' and was four years her junior. Both women were curious, keen travellers and intelligent, astute judges of character, self-educators with a strong visual sense, and an acquisitive love of beautiful things. Mrs Greville's homes in Mayfair and Surrey became a popular haunt of the new Queen Mary, who appreciated sympathetic female company and fine cuisine in opulent surroundings. '*Dear* Queen Mary,' Mrs Greville would purr whenever a royal visit was imminent, 'Always so welcome, but never any notice!'

As Princess May of Teck, she had been engaged to Prince Albert Victor, known as Eddy, the Duke of Clarence. However, in January 1892, Eddy died suddenly from pneumonia. An apparent tragedy may have been a narrow escape for both May and the Royal Family; dissolute and unreliable, Eddy would have been a dreadful husband and a worse monarch. Once a year's mourning had been observed, Prince George, now the heir to the throne, proposed marriage to his elder brother's former fiancée, and was accepted. Despite unpromising beginnings, their

marriage was a success. George adored his domestic life with, eventually, six children, in the cramped York House on the Sandringham Estate, where they had spent their honeymoon. May's creative impulses were stifled on marriage; George had ordered their first home to be completely furnished by Maples, a kind but misguided effort to save her any trouble. Understandably, she became the scourge of antique shops across the Home Counties, and York House gradually filled up with furniture and artefacts.

At Sandringham George was able to indulge his obsession with stamp collecting; on one occasion, his private secretary remarked, 'I see in *The Times* today that some damn fool has given fourteen hundred pounds for a single stamp at a private sale.' 'Yes,' replied Prince George, 'I am that damn fool.'

… long live the King'

George V acceded to the throne at a time when there was considerable social and industrial

Right: **Queen Mary was a frequent visitor to Polesden Lacey, especially on Sunday afternoons in the summer.**

unrest, with a newly emergent Labour party, and trouble brewing in Ireland. The new Queen Mary had the sense to see that social work and philanthropy were fields in which she could make a difference, and she applied herself to undertaking charitable works, and being seen to do so.

It is around this time that Mrs Greville and Queen Mary became firm friends rather than acquaintances. Mrs Ronnie had been associated with the 'fast set' around Edward VII, through her marriage and her twenty-year friendship with the Keppels. Now, the widowed Margaret was leading a blameless life. Furthermore, both Margaret and George Keppel had been friendly with Mary's younger brother, Prince Francis of Teck. He contracted pneumonia in October 1910, and was visited at home by George and Margaret; he did not pull through, but Mary was touched by their kindness.

Given their passion for jewellery, they may have found a common interest at the bedside of Prince Francis. He had been a notorious gambler, and had a mistress, the Countess of Kilmorey, known as Nellie. Francis had apparently given Nellie the Teck family jewels, known as the Cambridge Emeralds. After Francis's death, Queen Mary quietly bought them back for more than £10,000, and wore them at the Coronation the following year.

Mrs Greville was starting to enjoy life once more. Throughout the summer of 1912 she held dinner parties every Wednesday, and also attended soirées, balls and parties, mixing with royalty and the aristocracy. Unlike Mrs Keppel, who resolutely still wore black, Mrs Greville favoured white, cream, silver and gold, set off by some of her spectacular jewels. She had a diamond tiara and an emerald and diamond necklace, magnificent pearls, a set of black diamonds, and a wide bandeau of diamonds to be worn in the hair.

Throughout the summer of 1912 she held dinner parties every Wednesday, and also attended soirees, balls and parties, mixing with royalty and the aristocracy.

In August 1912 Mrs Greville was in Dublin for the annual Horse Show, and was a guest of the Earl and Countess of Aberdeen at the Vice-regal Lodge, a dance for 200 guests. She started to travel again and threw herself into socialising with a vengeance; she was at Cannes in January 1913 and, interestingly, she was described in a *Tatler* photo caption as Mr McEwan's daughter, not stepdaughter.

Death of Mr McEwan, 1913

In his latter years, Mr McEwan was described by Lady Sitwell as being '...so thin...as to look almost transparent...', and photographs of house parties show him as a slight, ethereal figure at the back of the group, in marked contrast to the well-upholstered forms of Edward VII and his court.

Mr McEwan remained physically active throughout his life, though his tastes were abstemious; 'My chief pleasures in life are walking and books', he told a journalist in 1896. In his final years William McEwan still travelled around London on foot whenever possible. Margaret Greville secretly employed a private detective to follow the frail old man to make sure that he managed to get safely across dangerous crossings. Despite these precautions, William McEwan was knocked down by a carriage and four horses near Hyde Park Corner. He died at his home, 16, Charles Street in London, on 12 May 1913, at the age of 85, with Mrs Greville at his side. She arranged for him to be buried in the churchyard of St Nicolas, the church she attended in Great Bookham, in a plot next to her husband Ronnie, rather than with Mrs McEwan in Highgate Cemetery.

At Mr McEwan's funeral, the mourners included Mrs Keppel, Lord Greville, and Margaret Greville's paternal cousins Robert and William Younger. Many villagers attended, their everyday clothes making a striking contrast with the formal black of the principal mourners. The oak coffin was carried by eight men from the Polesden Lacey estate, and the choir sang 'Peace, perfect peace'. A memorial service was held in Edinburgh at the same time, attended by representatives of the Corporation of Edinburgh, the university, the students' union, the Liberal Association, and the management and many of the employees from the brewery.

Deferential and lengthy obituaries appeared in various papers over the following days; *The Times* detailed Mr McEwan's commercial achievements but also recorded his philanthropy, particularly in Edinburgh: his 'tact and ability gained for him a personal influence to which few private members attain'. *The Guardian* made the point that he had a retiring and sensitive manner.

Mr McEwan's will

William McEwan was a very wealthy man; he was one of only seven British millionaires to die between 1913 and 1914, five of whom were Scottish. His fortune came to £1,503,940, worth approximately £65,000,000 today.

Mr McEwan owned 30 per cent of the shares in the Fountain Brewery, worth £326,250, and his investment in the Caledonian Railway Company alone was worth £88,400. He also had substantial holdings in mining and railway companies, particularly in America.

His will names Margaret Greville as 'the lawful daughter of me and Mrs Helen McEwan, my late wife…' This was a brave statement for the time, and he need not have made it. By doing so, he stated the facts of Margaret's parentage. It seems that to William McEwan the truth was more important, in the final analysis.

Below: **The Rt Hon. William McEwan, MP (1827–1913).**

Significantly, only nine days after Mr McEwan's death, on 21 May *The Times* was referring to 'his daughter, the Hon. Mrs Greville', rather than 'stepdaughter', in reporting on the will. Mr McEwan had arranged matters so that the truth would appear in the Establishment's paper of record, at a time when it would be unseemly to express titillated shock. Similarly, when she arranged to leave her houses and possessions to the nation on her own death, Margaret did so specifically in memory of 'My dear father, William McEwan', regardless of anyone's disapproval.

Mr McEwan appointed four trustees, including his daughter, and each was given £1,000 for administering his wishes. He left a bequest of £500 to each of the two managers and the secretary of William McEwan and Co., and a generous sum of £4,000 to his butler. The Royal Infirmary, Edinburgh, received £15,000; and a convalescent home associated with it benefited by a further £1,000. To his nephew Robert Younger, he left his house in Forth Street, Alloa, and 1,000 ordinary shares in the company. Robert's brother William received 7,000 ordinary shares; apart from a few other bequests, Mr McEwan left to Mrs Greville the whole of the remainder of the ordinary shares of the company belonging to him at the time of his death.

His will stated that money or property inherited from Mr McEwan's estate could not be seized or appropriated by any future spouse of Margaret. This was a specific provision and unusual for the time, and was a reference to the 1882 Married Women's Property Act. It was an attempt to protect her fortune if she should remarry.

Mrs Greville alone

In her father's memory, in June 1913 Mrs Greville gave the University of Edinburgh his substantial and elegant house, 25, Palmerston Place. Her gift was generous, but she felt no need to maintain any permanent base in the city where she had lived until her twenties. It would appear there was no contact between Margaret and the Andersons, though she maintained cordial relations with her Younger cousins, children of Mr McEwan's sister Janet, and some of the Grevilles.

Mrs Greville was now very much alone. The pleasure-seeking monarch she had cultivated for many years had died; within the past seven years she had also lost her mother, husband and father. She had no children, and she had severed her ties with the city of her birth, though she would visit occasionally for the rest of her life, to distribute *largesse* and to pursue her business investments. Even her dear friend and neighbour Lady Violet Savile had died the previous year.

In 1913 Margaret Greville was nearly 50 years old, and by the standards of the day a wealthy, childless widow might have been expected to retire quietly to her country estates, nurture her fortune and Pekingese dogs and take up needlepoint. But Mrs Greville was made of sterner stuff. The spur of grief, the public knowledge about her true origins, the inheritance of the lease on her father's magnificent house and sudden access to incredible wealth galvanised her. Yet again, she brought about her own metamorphosis.

After the death of Mr McEwan, Mrs Greville made some far-sighted decisions about the long-term ownership of Polesden Lacey. Cynics might say that she was prepared to use it as a bargaining chip to ingratiate herself with the Royal Family. On 25 May 1914 she wrote an emotional letter to King George V: '… the fact is that I am alone in the world, I love Polesden Lacey, I have nobody to bequeath it to and I can never forget King Edward's kindness to me, he helped me to face life. He was an angel to me and if Your Majesty would consent, I should feel so happy if one of his descendants lived here. I made a will last March extract (copy) of which I enclose…if Your Majesty disapproved of what I have done, to save trouble when I am gone I could revoke it – I left the sum of £300,000 to go with the place and an additional £50,000 for possible alterations…it is so sad to have nobody and I just can't bear to think Polesden may have to go the same way…'

Unsurprisingly, offered a windfall of £350,000 (the modern equivalent of more than £15 million) and a country estate for one of his children, the King replied promptly. He and the Queen visited Polesden Lacey on 14 June 1914 to tour the house and garden and discuss the matter. George V recorded in his diary: '…Mrs Ronny [sic] Greville gave us tea, she showed us all over her lovely house and gardens, a most charming place. She told me confidentially that she intends leaving the place to one of my sons with at least £300,000 to keep it up, to be selected by me and to belong to him and his descendants for ever. He will indeed be a lucky boy…'

They agreed that, as the Prince of Wales would inherit the Duchy of Cornwall, which would give him an impressive disposable income, Polesden Lacey should go to Prince Albert, the second son. From this time onwards, Mrs Greville showed a special interest in Bertie's welfare, and when he left the navy she would invite him to dinner and to stay for weekends. Their first encounter seems to have been over a lunch in March 1918; Queen Mary wrote to Bertie: 'I am glad the luncheon went off so well, I had such a nice letter from Mrs Greville, most kind and amiable so that I hope a good beginning has been made…'

From this time onwards, Mrs Greville showed a special interest in Bertie's welfare, and when he left the navy she would invite him to dinner and to stay for weekends.

In fact, the 'nice' letter from Mrs Greville to Queen Mary had been positively rapturous: 'He is delightful, such charming eyes, manners and complexion. His eyes simply exude kindness. I was so pleased...fancy a delightful young radiant being like that being so charming to me. I do love youth...he has promised to come again when he returns.' It would appear that at this stage the future ownership of Polesden Lacey was kept a secret from the Prince, but Margaret Greville and Queen Mary now had another common bond; providing a secure future for young Bertie.

Transforming 16, Charles Street

'A Gifted Hostess'
Mrs Ronald Greville is giving up her own house in Charles Street, Berkeley Square, London, and intends to take up her residence at the house in the same street that was occupied by her father, the late Mr William McEwan. It is a larger residence than her own, nevertheless she intends to add to it, and is having it entirely done up and redecorated so she evidently intends to take up active social life again. The decision will be warmly welcomed, since Mrs Greville is that rare thing, a born hostess, her gift for hospitality, as the late King Edward said, amounting to positive genius.

(Scots Pictorial, *13 September 1913*)

Mrs Greville decided to use her enormous fortune to create a suitable setting for a pre-eminent London hostess. She had always enjoyed proximity to power, and now she could wield it herself, by attracting politicians and entrepreneurs, royalty of all stripes and nationalities.

Mrs Greville had previously lived at No. 11 in the same street, but 16, Charles Street was larger and more impressive; a substantial terraced house built in 1753. The house was leased by Mr McEwan from the Berkeley Estate in 1892. The narrow road runs parallel to Piccadilly and at one end is Berkeley Square; lined with tall and elegant townhouses, it remains one of the most desirable addresses in central London. Number 16 is four storeys high, including the basement and attics, built of brown brick, with cast-iron railings and stone obelisk gate piers in front of the entrance. The double-doors at the entrance are made of oak and studded with iron, with an ornate fanlight above.

Once again, Mrs Greville employed Mewès and Davis, architects of the Ritz, who had transformed her country house, Polesden Lacey, blending the very latest in modern technology with an eclectic, revivalist style. The French influence was even more overt in their designs for Charles Street, though it incorporated neo-Georgian detailing where appropriate. Mrs Greville approved the plans in November 1913 and supervised the changes while living at 11, Charles Street. The remodelling work lasted from 1913 to 1914, and cost more than £17,000 (around £1 million today). Mewès died just before the outbreak of war in 1914; his partner Davis continued to oversee the final alterations to Charles Street, until he enlisted as an intelligence officer in the British army.

They were dealing with a restricted site; 16, Charles Street is a terraced house, opening straight onto the street, so they could not expand sideways. They devised an imaginative solution, extending the building at the rear to incorporate a modest former coach-house, whose entrance was in the parallel road running behind, Hay's Mews. In this structure they installed a massive, ornate ballroom, and above, a private apartment for Mrs Greville. Between the two blocks of the linked buildings they created an open-air courtyard, as well as an enclosed corridor linking the two sites.

Visitors arriving at the impressive entrance in Charles Street were ushered into the lobby, beyond which an ornate square staircase led up from the chequerboard marble floor to an octagonal ceiling light. The ground floor corridor, with its barrel-vaulted ceiling running to the back of the house, had various reception rooms leading off it. Sumptuous materials were employed: ornate rococo-style plasterwork ceilings, reclaimed historic fireplaces, a glorious, transplanted Renaissance-era Italian doorway decorating the inner courtyard, and coloured marbles for flooring. The breakfast room was fitted with a domed oval ceiling and latticed display cabinets; it was here that Mrs Greville displayed blue and white Chinese porcelain. Both breakfast room and morning room led onto the courtyard, accessible through half doors or French windows.

Visitors arriving at Charles Street were immediately received by a footman. A manservant was perpetually on duty at the front door to extend a welcome...

Left: **The imposing front door of 16, Charles Street in Mayfair, London.**

At first floor level, the barrel-vaulted corridor imitated a highly decorative Italian design, and a screen of marble Ionic columns led into the vast drawing room. This was impressively opulent, with panelled white walls, decorated with eighteenth-century gilded '*boiseries*' (ornate low-relief wooden carvings), probably salvaged from a French chateau. The high moulded ceiling was lit by huge crystal chandeliers, with candelabra side-lighting.

The ballroom that was constructed at the back of the house was executed in the grand Palladian style, with a deeply coved ceiling, and ornate columned and pedimented doorcases. The moulded ceiling was gilded with 18-carat gold leaf. Above were Mrs Greville's private apartments, similar in layout to the arrangement at Polesden Lacey, with a bedroom, sitting room, bathroom and maid's bedroom. There were six further guest bedrooms on the second floor. A second, less formal staircase gives access to all floors with a landing around an open classical gallery, a more domestic touch. Mrs Greville was an early pioneer of technological innovations, and had a lift installed, running from the basement to the second floor.

Staff quarters

The servants' quarters in the basement were accessed from the street by a discreet flight of steps at the front of the house. There was a fully equipped kitchen, and a large servants' hall, a combined sitting room and staff refectory. The steward's office was where the *major domo* was able to work in some privacy. The steward and the chef each had a bedroom in the basement, conveniently placed to guard the household silver in the nearby strong room. There was a pantry, a larder, a still room, a wine cellar and a serving room. The basement also housed the coal-fired boilers, providing copious warmth and hot water.

In Mrs Ronnie's day, the basement was a hive of activity, with the chef barking orders at the kitchen staff, the housekeeper marshalling the housemaids, and the butler chivvying the footmen. At the rear of the house, in Hay's Mews, was a line of former stables, converted to garages; here Mrs Greville's cars were housed at No. 11, and her chauffeur had a small apartment above. Female servants lived in the attic bedrooms above Charles Street. Senior female staff, such as her personal maid, housekeeper and secretary, each had a superior bedroom. The housekeeper was a permanent fixture, but most servants, including the butler and footmen, travelled between the two houses accompanying their mistress on her social round, making the trip in a motorbus bought for the purpose. In addition, she owned a motor-van, which delivered produce and flowers from the estate up to London.

A growing social circle

While the renovation continued, Mrs Greville continued to entertain guests at Polesden Lacey; as she cultivated a new social circle, the press gave her very benevolent coverage. A positively glowing account of her virtues survives in the press clippings album:

"The Hon. Mrs Ronald Greville is one of the women who is very wealthy, and in the first flight socially, and is yet devoid of enemies. This is rather odd because to be rich and socially successful seems to raise the gorge of a certain kind of woman and man who are neither… no house parties are more enjoyed than Mrs Ronnie Greville's; she has the real hospitable talent which secures guests' pleasure without worrying either herself or them. You have no idea how unusual a talent it is considered…"

(Lady's Pictorial, *1 August 1914*)

Mrs Greville moved into the London house at the end of November 1914 and, surrounded by her excellent paintings, Chinese ceramics and French furniture, began once again to entertain. At her first dinner party, the guests included the Prime Minister and Mrs Asquith, an indication that she was establishing herself among the principal political hostesses.

Collecting and patronage

Both father and daughter were serious collectors of art, and having inherited his house and collections in 1913, Margaret continued to buy. Mr McEwan had favoured seventeenth-century Dutch and Flemish paintings. He also sat for two portraits; the one by Benjamin Constant (1900) was executed in six sittings at the Savoy hotel, and he disliked it, although his daughter was very fond of it; the second portrait, by Walter Ouless (1901), he found more satisfactory.

His daughter's tastes in paintings were more eclectic – she collected early Flemish and Italian art. She may have been influenced by the *goût Duveen*, the taste of the important London art-dealer and subsequent benefactor Joseph Duveen, and she also bought through Agnew's. Margaret Greville particularly favoured portraits, especially of children, and was prepared to spend considerable sums to acquire important British paintings, such as Lawrence's *The Masters Pattison*. In later years she took the advice of Professor Tancred Borenius. Her most important paintings were on display in her London home; Polesden Lacey housed the less significant artworks, in keeping with its role as a more relaxed country house.

Above: **Mrs Ronnie collected miniature carved dogs.**

Mrs Greville's acquisitions were intended to make a superb setting for entertaining. She was also assembling the art and artefacts that hinted at a lengthy and respectable past for her antecedents; she may have had to buy her own furniture, but with her extraordinary wealth, she could afford to buy someone else's history. As James Lees-Milne from the National Trust noted on his first visit to Polesden Lacey in 1942, after her death: 'The interior was, I imagine, entirely refitted by Mrs Greville, in the expensive taste of an Edwardian millionairess. But it is not vulgar. It is filled with good things, and several museum pieces.'

Both her homes had copious collections of French and lacquered furniture, antique silver and museum-quality Renaissance-era majolica. In keeping with British tradition, she collected all sort of *objets d'art* from the Far East: jade and soapstone carvings, and porcelain of great intricacy. She was fond of *famille rose* and blue and white Chinese ceramics. Meissen was another favourite and it is believed that she even fed her favourite pet dogs from a Meissen bowl.

In addition, Mrs Greville's Edwardian heyday coincided with the era associated with Fabergé and, like many a society lady, Mrs Greville collected tiny carved animals with their jewelled eyes. The idea had originated with Mrs Keppel, who asked Fabergé to replicate the various animals in Queen Alexandra's zoo at Sandringham. Mrs Greville displayed her collection in a vitrine in her salon; she would draw the attention of guests to them and point out which pieces had been given to her by King Edward and which by other guests, '*so* generous', a heavy hint.

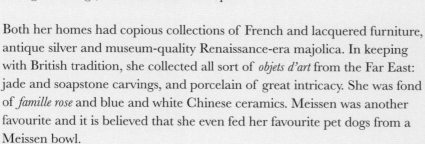

In keeping with British tradition, she collected all sort of objets d'art from the Far East: jade and soapstone carvings, and porcelain of great intricacy.

The Great War

There had been a certain amount of anti-German feeling among the upper classes, and frequent dire warnings about 'the coming German peril' from Lord Northcliffe, proprietor of *The Daily Mail*. Osbert Sitwell, already in the Grenadier Guards, recalled 1913 and 1914 as 'prosperous and gay', with parties and balls, country house weekends and ostentatious consumption of luxury. On the surface, all was well, yet in the summer of 1914 Sitwell detected a feverish mood of restlessness among his fellow officers.

"The postponed Court Ball, which you remember was put off when the Archduke Ferdinand and his wife were so cruelly murdered, took place on Thursday night and was, of course the last Court function of the season... Mrs Ronald Greville wore an immensely tall and very handsome tiara of diamonds and a magnificent necklace of sapphires and diamonds, and 'went on' to Court from a dinner at Mr and Mrs Walter Burns..."

(The Lady, *22 July 1914*)

The assassination of the Archduke Franz Ferdinand in Sarajevo on 28 June 1914 initially caused only a ripple in the newspapers, and the upper classes went ahead with their arrangements for the summer. A group of well-heeled Britons planned a house party, staying at the wonderful mansion of Clingendahl near The Hague. The party included Daisy, Baroness de Brienen; the Keppels; Violet, Duchess of Rutland; her daughter Lady Diana Manners; Harry Cust; Lord and Lady Ilchester; their great friend Maggie Greville; and her distant relation by marriage, Sir Sidney Greville. The house party was large; there were suitable young men to entertain Violet Keppel and Elizabeth Asquith, daughter of the Prime Minister, who arrived on 25 July.

Considering how well-connected all these guests were, it is perhaps ironic that they were surprised when Germany invaded Belgium. Urgent telegrams were dispatched from Britain in pursuit of friends and relatives abroad. The Clingendahl house party broke up, and the British guests packed hurriedly and headed for the Hook of Holland, hoping to get home on a chaotic and packed boat. It normally carried 100 passengers, but on the evening of 3 August it arrived at Harwich with 780 on board. The

Keppel family home had been closed up and no food was available, so George retreated to his club and Alice took her two young daughters for breakfast at the Ritz, a hotel which would become a bolthole for her in further times of trouble.

"I held a council at 10:45 (PM) to declare war with Germany, it is a terrible catastrophe but it is not our fault... Please God it may soon be over and that He will protect dear Bertie's life..."

(*King George V's diary, 4 August 1914*)

The outbreak of war shocked many; according to Nancy Mitford, one society lady remarked, 'But they can't have a war, there is nobody in Paris!' There was an initial burst of jingoistic flag-waving, with demonstrations of anti-German feeling; defenceless dachshunds owned by fashionable ladies had to be walked at night by footmen, to avoid unpleasantness. Vilification of 'the Hun' was whipped up by the popular press, with tales of German troops' atrocities against Belgian nuns and children. Prince Louis of Battenberg, First Sea Lord, was hounded from his post in October 1914, and in 1917 he changed the family name to Mountbatten. In 1917 King George V adopted the name of Windsor in order to confirm the Royal Family's loyalty to Britain, despite their many continental relations.

The war galvanised the Royal Family. On the first full day of the hostilities, 5 August 1914, Queen Mary wrote: 'Set to work to make plans to help the existing organisations with offers of clothing, money etc.' The Queen was committed to her charity work, and involved hundreds of thousands of volunteers. In September 1914 her appeal to raise funds to create work for women thrown out of employment by the war garnered £5,000 from William Waldorf Astor, £1,000 from Andrew Carnegie, and £100 from Mrs Greville.

In October 1914 the Joint War Committee, created by the British Red Cross and the Order of St John of Jerusalem, started fund-raising to provide relief for injured soldiers. Society hostesses offered their country homes to military patients; early in 1915 Mrs Greville opened the north and west sides of Polesden Lacey as a convalescent home linked to King Edward VII's Hospital for Officers, under

Ambulant patients were encouraged to exercise with a little croquet, golf or riding.

the watchful eye of Mr Bole, the Head Steward. Ambulant patients were encouraged to exercise with a little croquet, golf or riding.

The staff of nurses and orderlies lived on site, but Mrs Greville continued to entertain her regular circle of ambassadors, peers and politicians. The King and Queen paid a visit to the patients at Polesden Lacey on 7 August 1915. Queen Mary was leading by example in hospital visiting, in contrast to the general queasy avoidance of the horrors of war. She made it the duty of any well-placed woman with a conscience and an ability to organise. One footsore relative, trailing in her wake at one of these visits, protested, 'I'm tired, and I hate hospitals.' The Queen replied, 'You are a member of the British Royal Family. We are *never* tired and we all *love* hospitals.'

Meanwhile, Mrs Greville added to her charitable activities by helping to organise various events at her London house. She helped to run the Maple Leaf Club, which offered hospitality to Canadian soldiers during the Great War, making 11, Charles Street available for visiting servicemen. Queen Mary visited the club on 11 February 1917. 'It was very nice and informal. I shook hands with all the officers before leaving' she recorded in her diary. For her war work, Margaret Greville received a medal from the King and Queen.

Above: **In the early years of the Great War, Mrs Ronnie gave over part of Polesden Lacey to convalescent soldiers and medical staff.**

The war and Polesden

Life at Polesden changed markedly; in November 1915 Mrs Greville wrote to her Head Steward, Bole, asking him to thank all the staff who had made the military hospital so successful. She expressed her hopes that she would be able to reopen the convalescent facility in the future, but in the meantime she planned to pursue her war effort activities from her London base. Meanwhile, the golf course was ploughed up and potatoes planted. Mrs Greville's male staff joined up; unlike her contemporary Lady Sackville-West, who berated Lord Kitchener for conscripting her menservants, Mrs Greville recognised the need for soldiers. But there were some exceptions; she apparently offered to 'pull strings' to keep one of her young gardeners at home with his widowed mother, as he was her only child, but both mother and son declined her offer. So she kept his job open for him on his return; fortunately he survived. Meanwhile, she encouraged the estate staff to produce more food; Mr Prince, the Head Gardener, frequently exhibited award-winning Polesden Lacey vegetables.

Even in the depths of war, there were opportunities for Mrs Greville to indulge one of her lifelong interests, vicarious romance. She was a great matchmaker, and she would smooth the path of true love if it was possible. Fond of weddings, she could always be relied upon for a generous present if she approved of the match. She was also a practical support. Travelling in Europe was out of the question during the Great War, but in the summer of 1917 she lent Polesden Lacey in succession to two pairs of honeymooning couples, the Marquess and Marchioness of Carisbrooke, and Prince Alexander of Battenberg and his bride.

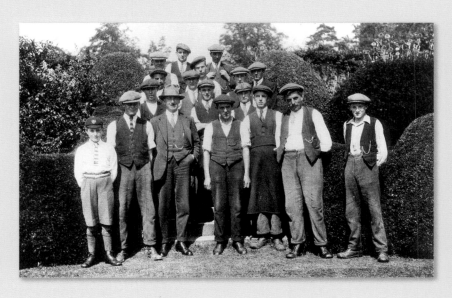

Below: **A group of the gardeners in the 1920s at Polesden Lacey.**

The end of the Great War

"I cannot let this day pass without sending a line to tell Your Majesties how I rejoice and how all these months I have admired the example, courage and valour of the King and Your Majesty which has so endeared you both to all and without whose glorious example this great end could not have been achieved..."

(*Letter from Margaret Greville to Queen Mary, Armistice Day, 11 November 1918*)

The First World War was a cataclysmic event; in total more than 9,000,000 had been killed, including 942,135 from the British Empire. It had ruined a generation, leaving children fatherless and women widowed. Most of Europe, Russia, Japan, Africa, the Middle East, the Far East, and even the United States had been dragged into the conflict. It had toppled dynasties and brought down the three imperial crowns of Austria, Germany and Russia. The Ottoman Empire had passed into history; Kaiser Wilhelm II had abdicated and gone to live in Holland; and Ireland was inching towards either independence or civil war. In a little over four years, the war had fatally undermined the crown of Greece, removed all power from the German princes, and brought about the Russian Revolution and the murder of their royal family.

The British and European ruling classes feared what Winston Churchill called 'the plague bacillus of Bolshevism'. They were aware that the proletariat could turn nasty. The returning soldiers, many of them mentally or physically damaged by their experiences, had lost the sense of deference they used to show their social superiors. Their jobs were now occupied by women, and in many cases the employers wished to keep them on. There was also the problem of 'surplus women', the wives and daughters of dead and injured troops who needed to earn a living, as well as unmarried women who did not care for a lonely, single future.

For some women the Armistice allowed them to carve out a new existence, one that was more outgoing and less hampered by the past. They were a financial force to be reckoned with; a number of wealthy, independent women were unaccountable to anyone. Mrs Ronnie Greville, widowed, orphaned, childless and 55 years old by Easter 1919, scooped up the convalescent demobbed officer and heir to a baronetcy, Captain Osbert Sitwell, and whisked him off to Monte Carlo in her Rolls-Royce for a long-overdue continental holiday.

Travel, Romance and the 1920s

"That intrepid traveller, Mrs Ronald Greville, has just returned from a five month trip abroad...there can be few corners of the civilised world Mrs Greville has not visited."

(Queen, *13 May 1925*)

Back to the Med

Captain Osbert Sitwell had met Mrs Greville in 1916 when he had been briefly engaged to Violet Keppel. In March 1919, when Osbert was 27 and recovering from Spanish flu, Mrs Greville took him on holiday to Monte Carlo and Biarritz. This was the first time he had been abroad for pleasure since 1914; he had served in the army throughout the hostilities, and was exhausted and depressed.

Like many returning to the Mediterranean after 50 months of darkness and privation, Osbert was enraptured by the sunlight, the sparkle on the sea, the smells of coffee, the exuberant vegetation. He also noticed the changes wrought by the war. The wealthy Russians had disappeared from Monte Carlo; their huge holiday villas lay empty, and their former mistresses were eking out a living with a spot of millinery or dress-making.

In 1919 the Monte Carlo Casino could not match its pre-war excitement, when great

Left: **Mrs Ronnie encouraged the romance between heiress Edwina Ashley and Lord Louis Mountbatten when they visited Polesden Lacey but she was a reluctant chaperone to the couple in India, as she doubted his motives.**

fortunes hung on the turn of a card or the roll of a dice, but Mrs Greville's wealth allowed them both to gamble decorously. After a few weeks, they moved on to Biarritz, and Sacheverell, Osbert's younger brother, joined them. He had come hotfoot from Paris, where he had been astounded by the painters of the *avant garde*. The brothers agreed to hold an exhibition in London the following summer, 1920, of the 'modern masters of Paris'. They left Biarritz for Madrid and Toledo on 28 March 1918.

Mrs Greville moved on to Paris, where she met her old friend, the American millionairess Grace Vanderbilt, described as 'the last of the gallant old hulks of New York Society' by the journalist Beverley Nichols. The two ladies motored out to Fontainebleau, for a sumptuous lunch of lobster and Chateau Yquem. On their return, bowling along a minor road, the back axle of their car broke and the chauffeur, Pierre, lost control, landing the car and its passengers in a ditch. Pierre was knocked unconscious, and Grace Vanderbilt wailed, 'Heavens, what are we to do?' Mrs Greville suggested that they should clamber out of the car, flag down the first driver to come along, and have Pierre taken to hospital.

'But suppose we were to be taken for two cocottes?' implored Mrs Vanderbilt, who like her fellow passenger was a stout party of some advanced years, and favoured sensible footwear. Picking a rogue nettle out of her rubies, Mrs Greville observed, 'I think, my dear, that we may take that risk'.

Sonia and Roland

For Christmas 1919 at Polesden Lacey, Mrs Greville invited Alice Keppel, her daughter Violet, and the latter's new husband, Denys Trefusis. Violet had married the unfortunate Denys under duress, but her affections lay elsewhere, in her long-standing and passionate relationship with Vita Sackville-West, and the pair were to run away to France in February 1920. Mrs Keppel recognised that the marriage had been a mistake, but she believed that Violet must try to make a success of it. The mood at Polesden was tense. Mrs Greville departed on 27 January for New York on the *Mauretania*, to stay with the Vanderbilts, and was therefore on the wrong continent when the emotional maelstrom erupted. The errant Vita and Violet were pursued to France by their respective husbands and persuaded to return. Mrs Greville was aware of the subsequent scandal and, on her return, took a suitably robust and worldly line.

Margaret's adored goddaughter, and Violet's younger sister, Sonia Keppel wished to marry the Honourable Roland Cubitt, but his family were less than keen. They had disapproved of Alice's adulterous relationship with the old King; they were also unwilling to have the scandalous Violet Trefusis's younger sister join the family. 'Rolie' was their fourth son and his three elder brothers had all been killed in the war.

'I only called to tell you that I do not consider that your son is good enough for my goddaughter.'

The family estate, Denbies, was only two miles from Polesden Lacey and Lord Ashcombe, Roland's father, was Deputy Lieutenant of Surrey. In this capacity, he and Margaret Greville had crossed swords before, and relations between the two households were frosty. So Lord Ashcombe was surprised when Mrs Greville's Rolls-Royce swept up the gravel drive, driven by a chauffeur and adorned by a footman. His butler informed him that his visitor did not wish to leave her car, so Lord Ashcombe went out to talk to her. In ringing tones, Mrs Greville announced, 'I only called to tell you that I do not consider that your son is good enough for my goddaughter.' And she swept off.

Meanwhile, Mrs Keppel used a poker-player's cunning on Lord Ashcombe, to lure him into committing an enormous sum of money to Sonia and Rolie. She asked him if he would match a notional sum of money that the Keppels were prepared to give to the young couple as a marriage gift. Lord Ashcombe was unaccustomed to dealing with financially astute women, so he jocularly agreed. Mrs Keppel then named an astonishingly high figure, and it was too late for him to back down.

The wedding of Sonia Keppel and the Hon. Roland Cubitt took place on 16 November 1920, at the Guards Chapel, Wellington Barracks, with an impressive list of guests. Out of habit, Sonia's old nanny told her not to make a fuss about her dress as 'No one will be looking at *you*'. Mrs Greville gave the bride a magnificent emerald ring as a wedding present. The couple honeymooned at the Old Manor House, Hove, lent by Sir Sidney Greville, before moving on to Lord Ashcombe's villa in the South of France.

Pursuing the Prince of Wales

Mrs Greville embarked on the P&O liner the SS *Morea* at Marseilles on 19 November 1921. She was 58 years old and heading for Bombay to start a three-month tour of the sub-Continent. She was going as the guest of the new Viceroy, Lord Reading, and her visit coincided with that of the glamorous playboy Prince of Wales, briefly later Edward VIII, whom she already knew but wished to cultivate further. Lord Reading had arrived in India as Viceroy in April 1921. He was born in London in 1860 as plain Rufus Isaacs, the son of a Jewish fruit importer. He was happily married to Alice, also Jewish, who suffered from ill-health. Rufus Isaacs was appointed Solicitor-General, then Attorney-General, as well as a Privy Councillor. He had been an acquaintance of Mrs Greville for a number of years, probably meeting through their mutual friend Sir Ernest Cassel, but it was only on her trip to India that their friendship blossomed, a relationship that remained important to her for the rest of her life.

Large parts of India had been under the direct control of the British Crown since 1858; much of the country consisted of hundreds of sovereign princely states, who ruled their own people under a feudal system, and saw their relationship with Britain as being primarily with the monarch, not with the government. As a result, the representative of the British rulers was known as the Governor-General and Viceroy of India.

Maharaja is Hindi for 'great ruler'; the Maharajas or princes of India were fabulously wealthy. They owned fleets of Rolls-Royces, lived in great luxury, possessed fabulous jewels and travelled extensively to avoid the hottest weather in the sub-Continent. Their children were educated at Eton and Harrow; they toured Europe with giant retinues, shopped remorselessly and stayed at the great hotels. They were urbane hosts and welcomed Mrs Greville as a personal friend of George V and Queen Mary. Many of those she met on this trip were later given reciprocal hospitality at her two homes.

The Prince of Wales arrived at Bombay on 17 November 1921. He was not an easy guest; he was petulant, and drank and smoked too much. One character in his entourage who could cajole him was his cousin Louis Mountbatten. The young naval officer had accompanied the Prince on his tour of Australasia in *HMS Renown* the previous year. Assigned to the party on their arrival was 'Fruity' Metcalfe, an Indian army officer who was a superb rider and polo player, popular with the maharajahs and a great social asset. Fruity, the Prince and Lord Louis were to become great friends.

Mrs Greville reached Bombay on 3 December 1921, and was immediately caught up in a dizzying whirl of social engagements, organised by the Vice-

Left: **The Prince of Wales, photographed in India with some of the 'bag' after a successful day's 'pig sticking' (hunting wild boar) during a Royal Tour of Asia in 1921–1922.**

regal staff at Government House. She faced a plethora of dinner parties, race-meetings, garden parties and travel. One account of the impression she made survives in the papers of Sir Conrad Corfield, who encountered her at the outset of her Indian tour:

Above: **The Maharaja of Cooch Behar extended hospitality to Mrs Ronnie during her visit to India.**

"A lady who spent some weeks at Vice-regal Lodge during the Prince of Wales' visit was Mrs Ronnie Greville. I had heard of her friendship with Royalty and her immense wealth. She certainly had jewels which a Maharaja would envy. At one Vice-regal dinner party in Calcutta she wore emeralds, which I find hard to describe except that they seemed to cover her from forehead to fingers. At a subsequent party she wore diamonds of equal magnificence and extent. When I congratulated her on their beauty, she asked me if I thought they were real. I said I was no expert but they looked real enough to me. She then told me that one set was real and the other false, but she never told anyone which and had never met anyone who could always guess right; she had copies made of each set, and had arranged with the insurance company always to travel with one set real and the other false and to change from one to the other for different journeys without letting anyone know. The Company had then agreed to a big reduction in the premium. So she was not only rich but prudent; she was also very good company."

The party embarked on a tour of various states, travelling by car or rail, starting with a trip to Bikanir to stay with the Maharaja. On 28 December a programme of 'Indian Entertainment' was given in honour of the party. The guests were treated to an evening of song and dance, including one number performed on naked swords and spear heads. His Excellency took the salute from the Camel Corps (the technical term being a 'trot past'), while Lady Reading and Mrs Greville watched from the open-topped Vice-regal car. Margaret Greville kept the British press informed of her movements. *The Sunday Herald* (12 February 1922) reported:

"Mrs Ronnie Greville is, I hear, having a royal time…she has been indulging in the usual 'Grand tour' during the cold weather. Recently she added a diamond-studded enamel bracelet to her jewel collection. Perhaps it would not be correct to describe her as an official Ambassadress, but more than one ruler of an Indian State has been gratified to receive messages showing that the King and Queen of England do not forget old friends."

Each host competed to impress the Vice-regal party. They visited Gajner, where the Maharaja's estate comprised an artificial mile-long lake created in the Rajputana desert, stocked to provide a massive duck shoot for the revered guests, who were accommodated in a silk-lined and carpeted *shamiana* or tent. They went on a shooting party to mark New Year 1922. Mrs Greville visited Udaipur, Jaipur and Baroda, where the Maharaja's family dined off gold plates, their guests off silver.

Mrs Greville's scheming

Mrs Greville was among the guests invited to dinner on 25 January at the Choumala Palace by the Nizam of Hyderabad, in honour of the Prince of Wales. The printed seating plan survives at Polesden Lacey, glued into an album. A lavish meal was served to guests seated at three very long tables, arranged end-to-end. The Prince of Wales was at the centre of the second table. The much-coveted seat directly opposite him had, according to the plan, been allocated to a Mrs Powell – but the printed name has been scored through and the words 'The Honourable Mrs Ronnie Greville' has been added in a neat hand.

This game of musical chairs cannot have been an accident; out of 220 printed names appearing on the seating plan, only 3 appear to have been changed at the last minute and, of those, only Mrs Greville appears to have benefited from enhanced proximity to the heir to the throne. One wonders how she managed to contrive this, and what the Prince, accustomed to flirting with charming married ladies, thought of finding himself opposite a 58-year-old widow, the dear friend of his disapproving parents.

...only Mrs Greville appears to have benefited from enhanced proximity to the heir to the throne.

Mrs Greville moved on to stay at Government House in Madras (now Chennai), and then travelled to Benares (now Varanasi), and Agra, visiting the Taj Mahal. By Sunday 12 February she was back in Delhi, where she rejoined the other guests who had been invited by the Readings to stay at the Vice-regal Lodge for the visit of the Prince of Wales. At the ball they danced the State Lancers, but neither the Prince of Wales nor Mrs Greville knew the steps, with resulting chaos.

Among the new arrivals was the young Edwina Ashley, who had travelled by train from Bombay, a gruelling journey of some 750 miles. Mrs Greville knew Edwina well; she had also known Edwina's late grandfather, Sir Ernest Cassel. Mrs Greville was aware that Edwina was now one of the wealthiest heiresses in Britain, and that a romance had sprung up between Louis Mountbatten and Edwina while they were still in England; Mrs Ronnie had been instrumental in helping it along.

...a romance had sprung up between Louis Mountbatten and Edwina while they were still in England; Mrs Ronnie had been instrumental in helping it along.

One of their encounters was at Polesden Lacey, where Mrs Greville had invited them both to a shooting weekend; photographs of them together appeared in *Tatler* on 26 October 1921. Lord Louis had suggested lightheartedly that Edwina might visit India while he was there. Edwina was 20 years old and resourceful; she borrowed enough to pay for the fare, and recruited a suitable chaperone from the ship's passengers, securing an invitation from the Vicereine, Lady Reading, who was an old friend of her great-aunt.

Margaret Greville was usually a great champion of young people's love affairs. However, by this time she had become very protective of the young heiress, doubting Mountbatten's sincerity, as Edwina was so wealthy, having inherited millions from her grandfather. The young couple took advantage of Mrs Greville's reluctant chaperonage, and by the evening of the Valentine's Day ball at the Vice-Royal Lodge, Louis Mountbatten had persuaded Edwina to 'sit out' the fifth dance with him. He asked her to marry him, and she agreed.

It was on 20 February in India that the couple finally revealed what must have been the worst-kept secret in Vice-regal history. 'We felt it was only fair to tell Their Exs about what had happened,' Louis breezily wrote, 'since they were looking after Edwina out here. We decided this yesterday, but first told Mrs Ronnie, since she had been our constant chaperone, when we had one at all, since we have been here.'

Mrs Greville's account is intriguing; she composed an anguished note to Lord Reading. 'Monday morning' is handwritten at the top; which dates it as 20 February, before the news of the couple's engagement was officially announced.

My dear Viceroy

*I am absolutely wretched about that child – I couldn't sleep a wink,
I have grave misgivings. They were both at me last night – & she will not
be reasonable, all I begged for was that no engagement should take place
now, in a year she would be sick of him.*

*She has promised me that she will not write home till she has seen you,
but she promised me she would do nothing here – I want time – this is
absolutely confidential only I feel she is being thrown to the wolves so
although it is mean of one to betray her confidence I feel you are the only
pillar of strength and if only that hungry mother of his is told she will be
bound round – and there will be no escape – his tone too last night has
upset me. He took the line he would talk his mother round but she would
not be too difficult. I said E. was the one prize and there was not a mother
in England who would not want her. I don't dislike him, but he is wily
and I am really wretched and very sore at her breaking her word to me.
And she looked so white-faced and motherless last night. Dear Viceroy
please insist on no engagement – I have failed ignominiously but you are
so strong. Bless you and forgive me*
[signed] Maggie Greville

It would appear that Lord Reading soothed her misgivings since, on her return
to Britain, Mrs Greville held a congratulatory dinner party for the
Mountbattens and 50 guests, including the Duke of York, at Charles Street,
followed by a dance for more than 300 people. The Prince of Wales was best
man at the Mountbattens' wedding on 18 July 1922. Many Indian guests
attended, friends from the recent tour; Mrs Greville arrived with the Maharani
of Cooch Behar, the latter resplendent in a beautiful sari. A formal photograph
of the wedding party has pride-of-place in the photo gallery at Polesden Lacey.

Mrs Greville remained on good terms with the
Mountbattens, often having them to stay. In a
gossipy letter to Lord Reading in August 1923
she wrote: 'I spent last weekend at Lympne at
Philip Sassoon's and Edwina and Dickie were
there – she gets lovelier every day and I am so
glad it seems to be going well.'

*'I spent last weekend at
Lympne at Philip Sassoon's
and Edwina and Dickie were
there – she gets lovelier every
day and I am so glad it
seems to be going well'.*

Furthering royal connections

Returning to Britain in June 1922 after a seven-month absence, Mrs Greville threw herself into the social round once more, focusing particularly on royalty. In July 1922 she was invested with her honour, Dame Commander of the British Empire, but perhaps uncharacteristically, she rarely used the title.

Alice Keppel had recently relinquished her London home and sold her address book to the American hostess Laura Corrigan, and was now largely living abroad. Mrs Greville was too social a creature to give up her proximity to power and, unlike Mrs Keppel, she could afford not to. She was also anxious to avoid being seen as 'left over from the last reign', in the memorable phrase of *1066 And All That*. She concentrated on cultivating the King and Queen and the younger royals.

Queen Mary was a frequent visitor, and would often telephone and invite herself to one of Mrs Greville's homes for tea the same day. Her diaries suggest that she favoured Polesden Lacey on hot Sunday afternoons. This was a source of great pride for Maggie, but the lack of notice could throw the household into a lather. She would ring for Bole, the Head Steward, and issue instructions to the kitchen, where sumptuous teas would be prepared. Mrs Greville was in charge of the Georgian silver teapots (Queen Mary preferred Indian to China tea), and guests would tuck in to muffins, scones, home-made jam and fresh Jersey cream from the herd on Home Farm. 'Mrs Greville is one of the few women with whom the Queen takes tea as a private individual, coming and going without even the companionship of a lady in waiting,' said the *Scots Pictorial*, 28 January 1922.

Below: **The Tea Room at Polesden Lacey, a favourite haunt of Queen Mary. 'Maggie's teas were terrific', recalled Beverley Nichols, 'with great Georgian teapots, and Indian and China, and muffins and cream cakes and silver kettles sending up their steam…'**

The royal romance

*"Her dance last week in Charles Street was a
kind of dream of princes and lovely women..."*

(Tatler, *27 December 1922*)

Mrs Greville had failed to charm the Prince of Wales, but she liked his
younger brother, the Duke of York. Prince Albert, known as Bertie, was shy,
sincere, and inclined to stammer when stressed. Mrs Greville cultivated the
younger son, inviting him to meet her other guests on a regular basis at
Polesden Lacey; rubbing shoulders with ambassadors and politicians, she felt,
could help him develop.

In 1914 Mrs Greville had agreed with the King and Queen that she would
leave Polesden Lacey to Bertie on her death. As the younger son, his need for a
country estate and the capital to support it was greater than that of the Prince
of Wales. According to King George V's diary, Bertie first visited the house on
10 August 1919, with his parents and sister, Princess Mary. In 1920 he joined a
weekend house party including Edwina Ashley, the Maharaja of Kapurthala,
Lord Londonderry, the Duke of Argyll and Grace Vanderbilt. 'His Royal
Highness is a great favourite with Mrs Greville, and is often her guest,' reported
the *Daily Mirror*. He liked her, as his grandfather had done, for her hospitality
and her capacity to amuse and entertain.

Bertie was keen on a young Scottish lady called Lady Elizabeth Bowes-Lyon.
She was small and pretty with a radiant smile, dark, slightly fluffy hair, and
a taste for traditional dress. She was the ninth child of the 14th Earl of
Strathmore and Kinghorne, and was brought up at Glamis Castle in Angus,
a baronial pile with a gory history. Bertie met Elizabeth on 10 June 1920, at a
dinner party in Grosvenor Square, when he asked his new equerry, the Hon.
James Stuart, to introduce him to the girl with whom James had been dancing.
James's family, the Earls of Moray, were near neighbours of the Strathmores,
and the two Scots were good friends. Bertie was instantly smitten.

Hints were dropped and Bertie's friends and family encouraged the courtship;
the earliest surviving letter from Elizabeth to Prince Albert, dated 13 December
1920, thanks him for his letter and states that she is looking forward to Mrs

Ronnie Greville's forthcoming party, though with some misgivings as she had not been to a 'proper' dinner party for months. Mrs Greville had used the excuse of Albert's twenty-fifth birthday on 14 December to give a party for him, and Elizabeth enjoyed it.

Queen Mary contrived a visit to Glamis and was impressed by Elizabeth, who was forced to play hostess for the day as her mother was unwell. Considering the recent war, it was more diplomatic for Bertie to choose a British bride, rather than one from the usual Germanic principalities. Meanwhile, Bertie pursued Elizabeth with ardour, but she was very fond of James Stuart. It was difficult for Stuart to remain as Bertie's equerry, as the two men were becoming rivals in love.

He accompanied Bertie to Polesden Lacey for the weekend of 2–4 July 1921, but the next time the Duke of York stayed at Polesden Lacey, on 9 August 1921, he was attended by Wing Commander Louis Greig, his great friend and confidante, who was aware of his feelings for Elizabeth. The Duke also stayed at Polesden for a shooting weekend in October 1921; it seems likely that he confided in his hostess, for she invited the young lady to further events where they might be thrown together.

Having previously said 'Mothers should never meddle in their children's love affairs', Queen Mary decided to act resolutely. James Stuart was made an offer he could not refuse by Sir Sidney Greville, elderly courtier and notorious royal fixer, a distant relative by marriage and old friend of Mrs Greville. James had the opportunity of a lifetime to go to America to learn the oil business; after a final visit to Glamis in January 1922, he found himself working as a rigger in the Oklahoma oilfields, and did not return till 1923. Meanwhile, Queen Mary had invited Elizabeth to be a bridesmaid at the wedding of Princess Mary to Lord Lascelles in February 1922, a considerable honour; the official photos of the wedding, taken a month after James's departure reveal seven cheerful bridesmaids and one small and very glum-looking individual.

With the field clear, Bertie pursued Elizabeth throughout 1922. On 13 December 1922 they were guests of Mrs Greville at a dinner and dance at Charles Street, Elizabeth wearing a dress of silver tissue. The dance was 'a very jolly affair' and Bertie's two favourite brothers, the Prince of Wales and Prince George, were among the many guests.

Bertie proposed twice, and was twice turned down. It seems that Elizabeth liked him greatly, but she had no desire to marry into the Royal Family; she already had wealth and a carefree life, and marriage would mean a loss of personal freedom. King George, ever tactful, told his son, 'You'll be a lucky fellow if she accepts you.' Bertie's attempts to woo Elizabeth did not go unnoticed; while it is not possible to trace the origin of the following report, the tone suggests Mrs Greville:

"The next 'Royal engagement' hinted at in a Sunday paper clearly refers to the Duke of York and Lady Elisabeth [sic] Bowes-Lyon, who were both dinner guests before the ball at Mrs Greville's London house last Wednesday. For some time people have coupled the names of these young people...rumour has it, however, that the young lady has not been at all anxious to make the royal alliance.

It would be interesting if the next royal engagement is associated with Mrs Ronald Greville's house. For the last one – that between Lord Louis Mountbatten and Miss Edwina Ashley – was really settled at Polesden Lacey..."

(The Star, *18 December 1922*)

Determined Bertie told his parents that he was going to propose to Elizabeth one last time. On 13 January 1923 he popped the question again, and this time Elizabeth said yes. Their engagement was announced in the Court Circular on 16 January 1923; 'There is not a man in England today that doesn't envy him. The clubs are in gloom,' wrote Sir Henry 'Chips' Channon, Conservative politician and author. Congratulations poured in from all sides. It had taken nearly three years for Bertie to secure his bride, but he had been determined. His older brother, the Prince of Wales, was to be similarly single-minded in securing marriage to the woman he onloved, though with results that caused massive upheaval to the Royal Family and the succession.

Plans for the royal honeymoon

As usual, Mrs Greville had escaped the British winter and she was in South Africa. On 29 March 1923 she dispatched a telegram to London, to her Head Steward, Bole, dynamic in its terseness and galvanising in its content:

DUKE OF YORK SPENDS HONEYMOON POLESDEN. SO GO PALACE SEE GREIG REGARDING ARRANGEMENTS. GREVILLE

An offer she had made to the young couple had been accepted, and she had just received confirmation. While Mrs Greville packed hurriedly to return to Britain, Bole was sent to discuss matters with Wing Commander Louis Greig, of the Duke of York's household. He was a lively and extrovert Glaswegian who had trained as a doctor, and a trusted friend and mentor to Bertie, who was fifteen years younger.

This was a considerable coup for Mrs Greville; her country home was deemed fit for a royal romance, and her very good friend, the second in line to the throne, son of the King-Emperor, and his new wife, wanted to start their married life at her country estate. Running a lodging house in Edinburgh really was a world away.

Below: **The Duke and Duchess of York leaving for their honeymoon at Polesden Lacey on 26 April 1923.**

The announcement from Buckingham Palace about the honeymoon appeared in the press on 4 April; with just over three weeks to go, and it was vital that Polesden Lacey should be at its very best. The admirable house staff swung into action like a well-oiled machine and *The Sketch* reported on the day before the wedding:

"Everything at Polesden Lacey has been perfectly arranged, in anticipation of the arrival of the Duke of York and his Duchess... a little sunshine is all that is needed to turn it into a peaceful fairyland ...it will be a novel sensation for them after these weeks of rush..."

(*25 April 1923*)

Mrs Greville made her house and staff available to the couple but she stayed at Charles Street, so that the newlyweds had some privacy. Arrangements were made so that their personal servants could attend them, but they could be largely left alone. They were to use the private suite designed for Edward VII, a pretty set of first-floor rooms on the southern side of the building, with glorious views across the valley, described as 'a peep of beautiful distance' by the Joseph Farington, who once owned the house.

The royal wedding

"Wet morning early, cleared later and the sun came out between showers. Bertie and Elizabeth were married in Westminster Abbey at 11.30 by the Archbishop of Canterbury. Beautiful service."

(*Queen Mary's diary, 26 April 1923*)

The marriage of the Duke of York and Elizabeth Bowes-Lyon was the first of a royal prince to be held at the Abbey for more than five centuries. The wedding was extremely popular with the public; the son of the King was marrying a British bride, one whose prettiness and modest manners had already captured many hearts. It was an opportunity for celebration, a moment to look forward with hope.

Under uncertain skies, King George and Queen Mary entered Westminster Abbey to the stirring tones of Elgar's *Imperial March*. The King and George, Duke of Kent were in naval uniform; Queen Mary glittered in crystal-covered ice blue and silver, set off by magnificent diamonds; while Queen Alexandra struck a suitably regal note in purple velvet and gold lace.

...the son of the King was marrying a British bride, one whose prettiness and modest manners had already captured many hearts.

Bertie wore the uniform of a Group Captain in the recently created Royal Air Force. Elizabeth wore a simple gown of ivory silk crepe, vaguely medieval in inspiration, with Queen Mary's flowing veil of Flanders lace held in place by a wreath of orange blossom, with a white rose of York on either temple. Round her neck was a single row of pearls. She walked up the aisle on the arm of her father, the Earl of Strathmore, and paused at the Tomb of the Unknown Warrior, placing her bouquet of white roses and heather on the memorial, in memory of her lost brother Fergus, who died at Loos in 1915, and all the war dead.

Above: **The newly married Duke and Duchess of York, relaxing on their honeymoon at Polesden Lacey, 1923.**

After the ceremony, there was an eight-course wedding breakfast at Buckingham Palace, before the family – King, Queen, Duke and Duchess of York – made an appearance on the Palace balcony, the first of many. Bertie and Elizabeth, now man and wife, were driven to Waterloo station in an open landau pulled by greys, showered with rose petals by the crowd, and took a train to Great Bookham, to begin their married life honeymooning at Polesden Lacey for a fortnight.

The train drew up at Bookham Station at 5.10pm, to be met by a reception party headed by the Chief Constable for Surrey and other notables, as well as 300 children waving flags and blossom. The Duke of York expressed his thanks for the welcome but explained that they were tired and asked if he might be excused saying more. The royal car took them to Polesden Lacey, a brief ride past hedgerows lined with estate workers loyally waving handkerchiefs, and away from public view.

Peace at last, and they enjoyed the unaccustomed seclusion of the house and grounds until Sunday 30 April, when they caused much local excitement by attending Great Bookham parish church. The Duke and Duchess arrived by car, and were escorted to the front pew, which was Mrs Greville's usual seat. They played golf on Mrs Greville's nine-hole course, and charming photographs survive of the couple relaxing on the estate, looking ridiculously young in their oversized tweeds and sensible footwear.

Cruising in the 1920s

"A fellow passenger, on one of the ships that Mrs Greville cruises on, told me she starts her journey by congratulating the captain on his fine ship, praising the steward on the excellence of his cuisine and complimenting the cabin stewardess on the freshness of the bed linen. On this particular occasion all these items were far below standard, but so ingratiating was the London society hostess that a special effort to improve was made by all the ship's company. Dame Margaret's amiable travelling might well be copied by all of us when we venture from these isles."

(The Daily Chronicle, *5 May 1928*)

Mrs Greville spent a large part of the 1920s travelling the world, often by ship, usually in the company of one of her trusted personal maids. She was well connected with the upper echelons of the Foreign Office, and also cultivated specific ambassadors so that she would be afforded every courtesy when she arrived at her destination.

She set off on 14 December 1923 via Toulon on the SS *Osterley* for Colombo in Ceylon (now Sri Lanka), Burma and Japan. While in Burma she was provided with a private train carriage containing a bedroom, sitting room, bathroom and maid's room, courtesy of the State Railways. She followed Lord Curzon's suggestion that China was not safe to visit, and returned on the SS *Naldera*, leaving Singapore in March 1924. The following year she opted for South America and sailed on 12 December 1924, not returning till April 1925. Mrs Greville and the Duke and Duchess of York met on a tour of Australia in 1927, but the visit soured Mrs Greville. She set out on the SS *Osterley*, a lengthy voyage, which did not begin well

Below: **An inveterate traveller, Mrs Ronnie returned from the Far East on the SS *Naldera* in 1924.**

P. & O. S. N. Co.

List of Passengers
by
P. & O. s.s. "Naldera"
leaving Singapore,
27th March, 1924.

due to bad weather, delaying her planned meetings with the Aga Khan at Toulon and Osbert Sitwell in Naples. Her trip was timed to overlap with that of the Duke and Duchess of York, and after spending a period in New Zealand she travelled extensively throughout Australia, having been provided with the use of a private carriage by the Chief Commissioner of Railways between 18 and 23 March 1927. However she was back at Admiralty House in Sydney Harbour on 26 March to witness the arrival of Bertie and Elizabeth.

The royal visit to Australia was a success, and the young couple were presented with three tons of toys for the infant Princess Elizabeth. By this point, Mrs Greville had set out back to Britain, and a supposed interview with her appeared in the Australian press, corruscating in her views of the Australian people. It was reported at length that Dame Margaret '...would not live among Australians for thousands of pounds. They are uncouth. They have no art and they take no interest at all in anything save their own municipal and state affairs.' It was similarly stated that Queen Mary had taken umbrage at Mrs Greville's remarks, and that the latter had retreated to her country estate.

The royal visit was a success, and the young couple were presented with three tons of toys for the infant Princess Elizabeth.

Mrs Greville denied this vehemently, cabling the Australian Prime Minister, Mr Bruce: 'On arrival here last night I was horrified to find that statements had been published while I was at sea, purporting to represent views expressed by me containing abuse of Australia and Australians. I have never entertained those opinions or made statements to that effect. On the contrary, I received nothing but the greatest kindness and courtesy throughout my stay in Australia and have the pleasantest recollections of my visit.'

Mrs Greville always contested that she had been misrepresented and the memory rankled; at a lunch at Lady Cunard's in 1934, Maggie Greville told Bruce Lockhart that a journalist in Sydney had misreported her views on the country. She claimed that she had not replied, but also that she had not forgiven; her father had left a provision in his will that she should never invest her money in Australian securities, and she intended to impose a similar condition on the heirs to her estate. This was a promise that she fulfilled.

Entertaining in the 1920s

"Mrs Greville is rich and hospitable. An invitation to one of her parties is an honour and, if refused, is liable, like a royal command, not to be repeated. Of course, you may never have the chance of refusing, but I thought I would warn you in case..."

(Daily Express, *13 July 1927*)

In 1923 Mrs Greville was 60, but that did not stop her from relentless competition with other well-heeled ladies keen to establish themselves as leaders of society. She threw herself into entertaining with gusto at both her properties; a typical example was the Italian Ball, hosted at short notice in May 1924, to raise money for the Italian Hospital. The ball was packed; Charles Street was clogged with the chauffeur-driven motors of the guests, while the pavements were covered with red carpets. Society couples fought to gain access; one reporter noted that 'many lovely frocks suffered; many of them literally torn to rags'.

Country weekends had a different rhythm – more intimate, because the group was smaller, yet in each other's company for longer. Polesden could accommodate eighteen visitors for a full house party, with seven self-contained suites and plenty of spare bedrooms and bathrooms, and one of its most attractive aspects was the mood of self-indulgent enjoyment Mrs Greville encouraged. At the weekends, guests rose late, coming downstairs around noon. The men would wear tweeds or lightweight suits, depending on the season, and lounge around reading newspapers, unless they felt like playing golf or tennis. The ladies would be freshly made-up and immaculately turned out by their maids.

Mrs Greville had originally instructed her architects to create a setting that 'I can entertain maharajahs in', and she welcomed visitors from all sorts of backgrounds, introducing the prime movers from overseas countries to the élite in London. Mindful of overseas guests' various dietary requirements, at Polesden Lacey Mrs Greville had erected a separate kitchen, known informally as 'the curry house' where her guests' cooks could prepare special food according to custom and religious mandates.

Society couples fought to gain access; one reporter noted that 'many lovely frocks suffered; many of them literally torn to rags'.

Christmas 1928 was spent at Polesden Lacey, and Mrs Greville continued to entertain the following year, maintaining a particular fondness for the Duke and Duchess of York, to whom she behaved like some sort of favoured aunt. She had written to Queen Mary a little time before, claiming that 'the Duke of York has entirely won my heart, and he fills a great gap in my life...'.

Typical is the dinner dance she gave for them in November 1929 at Charles Street. Dinner was served at one large table for 40 and there were also two smaller tables set up in the handsome green dining room. The following year, in November 1930, she gave a party at Charles Street for both the Queen of Spain and the two Infantas, with the Duke and Duchess of York, now proud parents of a second daughter, Margaret Rose.

Above: **The Duchess of York (left), later Queen Elizabeth, sitting out a tennis match with a companion on the courts at Polesden Lacey in the 1920s.**

Mrs Greville went to some lengths to represent herself as not only the friend of the highest in the land, past and present, but also as a wise woman of the world. According to an interview in the *Sunday Referee* of 29 January 1929, a hagiography of the first order:

"Great women are rare indeed, and to meet one is an experience never to be forgotten... One of the greatest women of the day and of yesterday is the Hon. Mrs Ronald Greville, the sister-in-law of Lord Greville ... of medium height, pleasant to look upon, with a quiet voice, rather heavy lidded eyes, with a humorous twinkle in them, one feels the influence of her marvellous personality at the first moment of meeting.

A deep understanding of human nature, a wide tolerance, and an all-embracing kindliness are shown in her expression and in her conversation...'There's so much kindness and goodness in the world, after all, don't you think?'"

Not everyone who knew Mrs Ronnie might agree with that statement.

The Servant Problem

"...I came back from Polesden yesterday night. It was like Jazz Night at the Palladium. All the butlers were drunk – since Maggie was ill – bobbing up every minute during dinner to offer the Duchess of York whisky."

(Osbert Sitwell, quoted in John Pearson's Façades*)*

Every aspect of Mrs Greville's life was managed by her servants. She employed a team of highly proficient people who, in the Edwardian manner, worked behind the scenes to ensure that both her households ran smoothly. There were also her senior servants, the 'front-of-house' staff, who welcomed guests, served at table, accompanied her overseas, cared for her possessions, managed her social diary and guarded her fabulous jewels.

By the standards of the time, Mrs Greville was generally considered kind and considerate; before the First World War, a time when many in service were becoming restive, Mrs Greville organised an annual ball for staff, tenants and local tradesmen at Polesden Lacey. There would be dancing and supper for about 120. She also provided a permanent staff social club, which was built on the north side of the Stable Courtyard, complete with a billiards table and lending library.

The servants were given a fair amount of latitude when Mrs Greville was either absent or had no guests, and as her visits to Polesden in the 1920s

Left: **Mrs Greville relied on her menservants, from left to right: Frank Bole, Head Steward; Sydney Smith, Head Chauffeur; and George Moss, Head Butler, c.1928.**

were largely confined to weekends, a fortnight for Ascot and a fortnight at Christmas, they had ample time to enjoy the estate themselves. Arthur Thompson, who started as a groom at Polesden Lacey in 1907, recalled in an interview that the servants would often have parties 'in the big house' when Mrs Greville was away and the red carpets had been rolled up and stored. He fondly remembered roller-skating races along the wooden-floored corridors.

Senior staff

Perhaps Mrs Greville's closest employee was her personal maid, Marie Adeline Liron. She was recruited in 1908 and was known to her face as 'Mademoiselle' or 'Aline', and behind her back as 'the Archduchess', for her dignity and poise. Mademoiselle was Mrs Greville's close and valued confidante, so much so that generous provision was made for her in her will. So close were the pair, and so fond of the dogs, that one of the gravestones in the pet cemetery was dedicated to Cho, a Pekingese born in 1908 who died in 1924: 'The ever lively companion of Margaret Greville and Adeline Liron who tended and loved him for 15 years and mourn his loss.'

Her 'rock' was Francis 'Frank' Bole, a man whose job title varied between Head Steward, Groom of the Chambers and Head Butler. He stayed with her for more than four decades, and she frequently wrote letters and postcards to him from her travels, when she hadn't taken him along as her manservant. She was concerned enough about his health to have him seen by specialist doctors, and in her introductory letter to a physician described Mr Bole as 'really one of my best friends'. It was Francis Bole who, after Mrs Greville had died, destroyed her private papers as she had requested, and she made substantial provision for him in her will.

Her favourite butler was Bacon, and he claimed to be a communist. Bacon was a short, broad, maverick character, prone to drinking any alcohol available. It was almost certainly Bacon who excelled himself at a grand dinner for 25 people in honour of Queen Juliana of The Netherlands. The 9th Earl of Portsmouth recalled how the rotund butler had evidently been drinking. He bent to serve a silver dish of fluffy *pommes gauffrettes* to Mrs Ronnie, then suddenly belched with spectacular effect, sending a shower of potato into his mistress's hair and Queen Juliana's lap, and providing a liberal dusting to the magnificent centrepiece of hothouse grapes, pears and pineapples. 'There was a well-bred hush, but not before I, the youngest there, had broken into a nervous yokel's guffaw,' recalled the 9th Earl.

He bent to serve a silver dish of fluffy pommes gauffrettes to Mrs Ronnie, then suddenly belched with spectacular effect, sending a shower of potato into his mistress's hair and Queen Juliana's lap...

One evening at Polesden Lacey, it was apparent that a manservant serving at dinner was tipsy. Mrs Greville wrote a note, "You are drunk. Leave the room at once", and beckoned the man over. He placed the note on a silver salver, bowed to his employer, and lurched to the other end of the table, where he presented it to the guest of honour, who spent the rest of the meal in mystified silence. But there are many versions of this story; reliable eyewitnesses on different occasions insisted that the VIP victim was Sir John Simon, Sir Robert Horne, Sir Austen Chamberlain or even Lady Chamberlain. Perhaps these lapses of etiquette were regular occurrences; Mrs Greville may have given her indulged and intoxicated butler a warning note more than once, and each time he roguishly passed it onto some startled guest. Her favourite staff were certainly allowed agreat deal of latitude.

Junior staff

Mrs Greville's senior menservants often stayed with her for many years and she rewarded their loyalty. More humble employees were not so keen; Alf Wesley, third chauffeur at Polesden between 1929 and 1937, recalled that 'any sight of her made everybody scuttle like hell'. Alf's main role was to transport the servants between the two houses in the motorbus, following their mistress's peripatetic social life. He also helped man the Polesden Lacey fire engine. The Polesden Lacey Firemen received a small extra payment, typically two shillings per week for this duty, with three shillings for the head fireman. Two shillings would buy 40 cigarettes in the early 1930s.

The juvenile male staff, and boys belonging to the various estate families, also acted as caddies for visiting golf enthusiasts keen to go round the nine-hole course. They earned generous tips from the golfers, including Sir John Simon, Neville Chamberlain, Sir Philip Sassoon, Winston Churchill and the Aga Khan. The Duke and Duchess of York were fondly remembered by Robert Nash, son of the estate engineer; in the early 1930s they tipped him a shilling every time he caddied for them, and with the proceeds he was able to buy a bicycle for £3 19s 6d.

After the First World War, when it became difficult to get servants, Mrs Greville's ample fortune secured the best applicants, and the core staff at Polesden remained about 70, most of them employed on the estate, with a largely female staff in the house. Mrs Greville chose maids on the basis of their height and good looks. A junior housemaid joining the household at Charles Street in 1925 would start on £22 per annum, although one-third of that amount, totalling £7 16s a year, would be held back to cover the cost of the maid's laundry, which seems punitive.

She was not always willing to lose a trusted servant to marriage; she had a favourite personal maid, Gertie Hulton, who had been with her for at least three years, and accompanied her on occasional foreign trips. Gertie, tall, elegant and personable, flitted between Polesden Lacey and Charles Street in attendance on her mistress between 1928 and 1931, but was very discreet about what she saw; even after Mrs Greville's death, Gertie kept her secrets. However, like the other servants, she apparently relished watching the guests arriving in their finery. Mrs Greville often gave Gertie and her younger sister theatre tickets so that they could have nights out together, and passed on her garments and accessories.

In 1931 Gertie announced that she intended to marry. Her daughter, Sue Lovett, recalls: 'Mrs Greville was very fond of my mother, and did not want her to marry, as she wanted to keep her for herself. She said that my mother would not like washing her own floors – as though that was the only reason she should not get married.' Nevertheless, Gertie was adamant, and Mrs Greville, recognising the sincerity of her wishes, gave her blessings, and provided some practical help:

"Democracy 'Rolls' On
The Hon. Mrs Greville's second maid, Miss
Gertie Hulton, was married at St George's
church, Hanover Square. Mrs Greville
went to the wedding in a taxicab, having
lent the bride her Rolls."

(Liverpool Echo, *5 October 1931*)

Mrs Greville employed a succession of highly competent female secretaries who travelled with her, attended to her correspondence and assisted in organising her social life. In 1925 this post was occupied by Miss May Mombert. From 1930 to 1933 Miss Lysaght-Griffen was the secretary and Comptroller of Household, with responsibility for a household budget of £10,000 and a very good salary for the era, of £550 p.a.

Cuisine

Although tolerant of human lapses, Mrs Greville's standards were uncompromisingly high when it came to food and wine. The cuisine at both Polesden Lacey and Charles Street (French, of course) was 'unsurpassed anywhere', according to the *Daily Telegraph* in 1930.

Below: The dining room at Polesden Lacey is in late Neo-classical style and hung with crimson silk brocade. The mahogany chairs are in Chippendale style.

Mrs Greville was unusual in employing female cooks as well as male chefs. A typical 'find' of hers was Mrs Isabella Menzies. Mrs Menzies' mother encouraged an early taste for cookery, sending her daughter to a well-known cookery school in Edinburgh. Isabella's first job as a cook was at Polesden Lacey, a demanding role in an era where a dozen or so people sat down every day for luncheon or dinner, with five or six courses. A country-house cook had to have a considerable range of dishes in her repertoire. Mrs Menzies recalled 'hard work all the time', but also said that Mrs Greville was considerate to her staff. When she dined out at the Ritz and came across a new dish, she would arrange for Mrs Menzies to learn the method.

> *'Poaching' staff was not common in the 1920s and 1930s, but excellent servants were definitely at a premium.*

Retaining staff

On one occasion Mrs Greville suspected that Grace Vanderbilt was keen to 'poach' the services of the Archduchess, a suggestion she dismissed with a snort, saying, '…it is not a question of money. I don't believe the Archduchess would leave me even if Gracie were to offer her a million dollars. Poor Gracie! Such a snob. And like all Americans, no sense of proportion.' 'Poaching' staff was not common in the 1920s and 1930s, but excellent servants were definitely at a premium. Attempts to swipe Aunt Agatha's chef Anatole, as portrayed in the tales of P.G. Wodehouse, did have an element of fact behind them.

"The hostesses of the twenties were like great galleons, sailing the social seas with all flags flying and all guns manned, relentlessly pursuing their charted course – and not above indulging in a little piracy if the occasion demanded it. Those were days when women really did ensnare each other's chefs and kidnap each other's head gardeners, and offer the most shameless bribes to each other's 'treasures'"

(*Beverley Nichols*, Sweet and Twenties, p. 79)

Society Hostesses

"...the secret of her success as a hostess is two-fold. She has vivacity and a multitude of interests. And she is interested in everything, from politics to housing schemes – from museums to the theatre. She has gentle eyes and hair that is very thick and profuse...in any party Mrs Ronald Greville is an outstanding figure. She has emeralds that once belonged, I believe, to the Empress Josephine. Her string of pearls falls almost to her waist. Above all she is a great mistress of the art of conversation. That is why her dinner parties attract such distinguished men and women."

(The Times, *12 June 1934*)

Competition was fierce between the great hostesses of the London circuit in the 1920s and 1930s. With honeyed tones and decked out in diamonds, they competed to attract the most desirable guests to their dinner parties, ballrooms and intellectual salons.

Many of the best-known hostesses in the inter-war era were American in origin: Lady Astor, Lady Granard, Lady Cunard, Lady Mendl and Mrs Laura Corrigan. A few British-born women also forged their own social circles. Lady Sybil Colefax was described as 'a snob for brains', genuinely interested in talented people in every walk of life.

Dame Margaret Greville courted the politically powerful and royalty, resolutely claiming: 'I'd rather be a beeress than a peeress.' Her main rival was Lady Emerald Cunard, born plain Maud Burke in San Francisco. She had married Sir Bache Cunard, but the marriage was not a success; they had one child, Nancy, who led a bohemian life in Paris. After having been discovered in bed with her lover, the conductor and impresario Sir Thomas Beecham, Lady Cunard decamped from rural Leicestershire to London in 1911. After her husband's death in 1925 she changed her name to Emerald, the name of her favourite gemstone.

"To compare Lady Cunard with Mrs Ronnie Greville would be like comparing a butterfly with a bison. These two great social rivals – who needless to say, detested one another – had nothing whatever in common. Everything about Maggie Greville was solid, everything about Emerald Cunard was insubstantial..."

(*Beverley Nichols*, Sweet and Twenties, *p. 79*)

Emerald was often described as 'birdlike'; men were more complimentary than women. Oswald Mosley saw her as 'a bird of paradise'. 'The yellow canary of prey,' harrumphed Mrs Greville, spitefully.

***Opposite*: Lady Cunard at a ball in 1931, with the Maharajah of Alwar.**

London's hostesses monitored each other through the social columns of the newspapers, and Emerald was an occasional guest at Charles Street and Polesden Lacey. Mrs Greville adopted a tone of lofty superiority in speaking of her cosmetically enhanced rival; she would purr, '*Dear* Lady Cunard; I am always telling Queen Mary that she is not as bad as she is painted.' Emerald countered by spreading the rumour that Mrs Greville's cook used a bicycle pump to inflate the quail served at her table.

Mrs Greville had a low opinion of the American hostess Laura Corrigan, wife of an affable steel magnate. Rich Mrs Corrigan took over cash-strapped Mrs Keppel's beautiful house in Grosvenor Street, together with its excellent cook and butler and, crucially, Alice's address book. Mrs Corrigan tried to invite Mrs Greville to dinner; Maggie resisted, not wishing to grace another mature millionairess's table. 'I am never hungry enough,' she said. By chance, the ladies met at Lady Mendl's house in Paris, where Mrs Corrigan snubbed Mrs Greville. This gave Maggie *carte blanche* to relate the incident as an example of Mrs Corrigan's irreparable gaucheness. 'She may be charming – I'm sure she is – I do *not* say unkind things about people – but I did not wish to know her. I was also shortly going to America and I knew that if I could arrive in New York saying I did not know Mrs Corrigan, my stock would go up at once.'

Mrs Greville's social circle

Although past middle-age, Mrs Greville enjoyed the company of young people. This was the decade when the generation who had been too young to fight in the war erupted with artificially high spirits. The Bright Young Things indulged in pranks, stunts, fancy dress parties, juvenile party games, illegal nightclubs, intoxicants and sexual experimentation. Their mascots were the Prince of Wales, known to his family as David, and his younger brother the Duke of Kent.

'Whatever else may be said against the twenties, they were not grey; the whole decade is drenched in colour,' remarked Beverley Nichols, the handsome and precocious writer and journalist. Mrs Ronnie invited him often to her parties and to stay at Polesden Lacey. She gave him the nickname 'Twenty-Five', the title of his successful book of essays and portraits, published in 1926. He moved in celebrity circles, interviewing many of the popular figures of the day, from Dame Nellie Melba and Charlie Chaplin to Frank Sinatra. He was an early advocate for less hypocrisy about homosexuality, a courageous stance at that time.

Among Nichols's contemporaries and Mrs Greville's social circle were the Sitwell siblings, Osbert, Sacheverell and Edith, who had startled London with a strange blend of Futurism, Cubism and Dadaism. Inevitably, their literary efforts and Edith's performances attracted ridicule, but Mrs Greville stuck with them – in 1927 they launched a revue called *All At Sea*, sticking a rapier into the ribs of their old enemies. The audience included many of the Bright Young Things, such as Stephen Tennant, Cecil Beaton and Zita Jungmann, and Mrs Ronnie held a supper party at Charles Street after the first performance.

In general, Mrs Greville maintained a robust anti-intellectualism; she found the Sitwells acceptable because of their aristocratic background, but she favoured a more middlebrow approach to culture. Mrs Greville claimed, 'My dear, I know I am not an educated woman', tending to see a grand piano as a convenient setting for autographed royal portraits in ornate silver frames, rather than as a musical instrument.

Margaret Greville may have gravitated towards the powerful rather than the creative, but she harboured a life-long fondness for eccentrics. One of the many 'confirmed bachelors' who amused Maggie was Gerald, Lord Berners. A wealthy aesthete with exquisite taste and a wicked sense of humour, he was the model for Nancy Mitford's creation Lord Merlin, in *Love in a Cold Climate*. He appreciated Margaret Greville's 'unusual cattiness' and excellent cuisine. Gerald was a frequent guest at Polesden.

Henry Harris, known as 'Bogey' Harris, was devoted to Mrs Greville; according to her surviving guest books, he dined, lunched or stayed the weekend with her at either Charles Street or Polesden Lacey 75 times between June 1926 and August 1940. 'Bogey' had inherited a large fortune and was part of the Marlborough House Set. He was particularly fond of majolica, a taste he shared with Maggie Greville, and drove a hard bargain; both of them were remembered by friends on separate occasions as saying 'I hate waste. I'm Scotch, you see.' He said of Mrs Greville, '…one can live without everyone really, everyone but Maggie; she's like dram drinking.'

Mrs Greville and fashion in the 1920s

Mrs Greville was a woman of substance, and she was expected to take an interest in her appearance. Yet she did not suffer from vanity, and had few illusions about her looks. Professional studio portraits of her at this time show a touch of lipstick and powder, but she avoided any cosmetics in daily life. Mrs Greville was described by Beverley Nichols as '…a stout, grey-haired woman of no great beauty, though she had pretty hands and feet and a good complexion…'

Modern dress of the 1920s did not suit Mrs Greville's shorter, broader figure. Many critics welcomed the demise of rigid corsetry, choking high collars and pavement-sweeping trains of earlier years, but there were reasonable misgivings that straight dresses only flattered the female torso if it was similarly tubular. Daphne Fielding in *The Duchess of Jermyn Street* wrote slightingly of '…dumpy Mrs Ronald Greville, who might easily have been mistaken for the cook.' However, no one who had seen Mrs Greville in evening attire, festooned with gems, would have mistaken her for a servant.

Below: **Queen Elizabeth, the Queen Mother, wearing the Greville Tiara, prepares to celebrate her 75th birthday.**

Jewellery

"Mrs Greville is one of the few women who can wear jewels and yet not be outshone. It is a rare gift."

(The Surrey Advertiser, *25 July 1923*)

Mrs Greville adored jewellery and throughout her life she collected spectacular examples. She was a regular customer of Cartier, and between 1899 and 1925, Mrs Greville's name recurs in the Boucheron archives more than 60 times. Each year, except during the First World War, she would have her string of 210 pearls and her three necklaces restrung. Her Boucheron diamond tiara was remade at least four times to meet changing fashions, starting in November 1901, when it was in the form of a circular crown, entirely composed of diamond motifs on a platinum frame in the shape of papyrus leaves. It was designed to sit around a voluminous *chignon*, to be worn at Edward VII's Coronation the following year. In 1921 the tiara was remodelled by Lucien Hirtz to create a more compact, geometric bandeau design. This was Mrs Greville's favourite piece, and though slightly modified it became one of the most memorable pieces now in the ownership of the Royal Family.

Mrs Greville was a serious collector of magnificent jewellery, and she favoured jewels that had belonged to prominent women in history. Provenance mattered greatly to her, and she acquired Marie Antoinette's diamond necklace, the Empress Josephine's emeralds and diamonds, and a diamond ring that had once belonged to Catherine the Great. She also commissioned new pieces from the greatest jewellers of the day.

Mrs Greville was highly competitive about jewels. During a dinner at Charles Street, one of her American guests had lost the central diamond from her necklace. All the other guests scrabbled to look for the stone, which, no doubt, had fallen onto the carpet of her immense salon. Margaret Greville, seated in her armchair, handed a magnifying glass to one of the gentlemen present, saying, 'Perhaps this may be of assistance?', implying that it was such a tiny stone.

Asked to give her opinion on Lady Granard's famous pearls, she dismissed them with a shudder saying, 'I thought it better not to look.' On another occasion she and Mrs Arthur James attended the same ball. Both women were sporting lovely strings of pearls, but Maggie observed that Mrs James was showing four rows of pearls, while she appeared to be wearing only three. Undaunted, she adjusted her cleavage and produced a second set of pearls, a further three rows, making a total of six.

"You must think that I dislike Lady Cunard, I'm always telling Queen Mary that she isn't half as bad as she is painted".

Money matters

"She was walking down Regent Street one day and she saw a Ford van in the window. 'Such a pretty little affair, my dear…and I always admired Mr Ford, even though he trod on one's feet when he made one do those extraordinary square dances. I always carry a little loose money in my bag' – (the Ford, in those days, was about £600) – 'so I went in and bought it for cash.' She put her hand on my arm. 'Always pay cash, my dear … it always pays."

(*Beverley Nichols*, Sweet and Twenties, *pp. 82–3*)

Mrs Greville's attitude to money was slightly schizophrenic, perhaps as a natural reaction to her frugal upbringing; she enjoyed using it as bait for the people she wished to impress. She had a reputation for financial shrewdness, and anyone who cultivated her, hoping to get near her considerable fortune, found they were wasting their time. Instead of spreading financial largesse, Mrs Greville spent enormous sums on her two houses, their staff, contents and cuisine, in order to attract those she wanted to draw into her circle.

Beverley Nichols described her as 'an extraordinary mixture of Scottish cautiousness and golden-hearted generosity.' She would promise every year to have delivered to her friends a crate of the beer specially brewed for Edward VII, yet this never materialised. Though generous to newlyweds, she resisted giving presents when they might be expected. Famously, one Christmas Eve at Polesden Lacey, Nichols received a small present, a paper-knife made of jade, in a slightly battered satin-lined case. Lady Chamberlain, who witnessed this, was outraged – Mrs Greville had 'recycled' the carefully chosen present she had given her three years before.

> **Beverley Nichols described her as 'an extraordinary mixture of Scottish cautiousness and golden-hearted generosity.'**

Yet she was a considerable donor to charities and good causes, and did not seek to advertise her gifts. She retained an interest in medical research; in memory of Ronnie, she funded a Guy's Hospital scholarship for research into cancer. She paid for the appointment of a research lecturer in pharmacology in 1914, and was active in charity efforts in London's East End, including providing free milk for poor schoolchildren.

Mrs Ronnie continued a philanthropic scheme set up by her father and an Edinburgh lawyer in the 1880s, to assist students too poor to attend the evening classes at Heriot Watt University or the Edinburgh College of Art. Mrs Greville funded the studies of between 200 and 300 students a year on the McEwan-Pretsell programme until 1940. She also contributed to the extension programme of the college, especially the improvement of the library, and would visit the university to meet the students at the beginning of each academic year.

Well known as a wealthy woman, she received frequent requests for help. She developed a standard response to be sent to them, in the form of a typed letter:

Dear
For the following reasons, I am unable to meet your demands. I have been held up, held down, sand bagged, walked on, sat on, flattened out and squeezed by the Income Tax, Super Tax, Tobacco Tax, Beer Tax, Motor Tax, Purchase Tax and every Society, Organisation, and Club that the inventive mind of man can summon up for the Red Cross, Double Cross and every bloody cross and hospital in this country.

The Government has governed my business until I do not know who the hell owns it. I am inspected, suspected, examined, informed, required and condemned so that I don't know who I am, where I am. I am supposed to have an inexhaustible supply of money for every need, desire or hope for the Human Race, and because I will not beg, borrow or steal money to give away, I am cursed, discussed, boycotted, talked to, talked at, talked about, held up, rung up, robbed and damned near ruined.

The only reason I am clinging to life at all is to see what the bloody hell happens next.
I am,
Yours faithfully, etc…

The brewery

Mrs Greville retained ownership of 30 per cent of the McEwan brewery company shares, and although never a director, would occasionally summon the board members to Polesden for meetings. Kenneth Clark recalled how the board would emerge pale and shaken after their encounter with Mrs Ronnie.

William McEwan Younger, born in 1905 and named after his great-uncle, went into the family firm in 1928. Part of his business training was conducted in London, and he stayed at Mrs Greville's house in Charles Street, enjoying both the unqualified luxury and the social life. Margaret Greville was impressed by Bill, and when she died she left him all her ordinary shares, making him a very rich man.

The worldwide economic crisis of the early 1930s had major ramifications for the wealthy as well as the hard-pressed. However, this crisis made British exports more competitive in overseas markets; a boon to manufacturers such as brewers. There was still some snobbery about wealth gained from trade; Oswald Mosley remarked of Mrs Greville, 'Appropriately enough she looked like a blousy old barmaid.' However, there was much worried talk among the moneyed classes and many in society were shaken by the fragility of their apparent wealth. Others, like Mrs Greville, while complaining vociferously about the crisis, were well placed to ride out the storm.

Entertaining royalty

"...no hostess stands higher in the esteem of the Royal Family..."

(Evening News, *30 June 1933*)

Mrs Greville was partial to blue blood. When Lady Strathmore, mother of Elizabeth Bowes-Lyon, remarked that certain people 'have to be fed royalty like sea lions fish', she probably had Mrs Ronnie in mind. Mrs Greville boasted to Kenneth Clark that she had had three kings sitting on her bed in a single morning.

Her campaign to charm the Prince of Wales foundered and he let it be known to hostesses that he found her 'a bore', but her 'royal collection' was not confined to Britain; she was internationalist in her interests. In July 1923 she threw a grand dinner at Charles Street for a large number of Indian princes and maharajahs as recompense for their hospitality the previous year. In July 1927 King Faud of Egypt dined with her. She socialised with the King of

She boasted to Kenneth Clark that she had had three kings sitting on her bed in a single morning.

Greece, having him to dinner in July 1933, and she was a guest of the Duke and Duchess of Sutherland, when they hosted a visit by King Feisal of Iraq. She also had a lengthy friendship with British-born Queen Ena of Spain. Maggie was always keen to drop her name wherever possible. A visiting card survives with her name and address printed on one side and a hand-written note on the reverse to Gladys, Duchess of Marlborough, reading: 'Will you both come in tomorrow (Thursday) night at 10:30. Wee, wee party for Queen of Spain.' Another handwritten note reads: 'Will you not come to a little dance which I am giving Tuesday 1st July 10 o'clock to meet Their Majesties the King and Queen of Spain. RSVP, decorations.'

Above: **Her Majesty the Queen of Spain and HRH Prince Henry playing tennis on the Polesden Lacey tennis courts, 16 July 1926.**

Mrs Greville was helpful financially when Ena and her husband lost their thrones. Harold Nicolson mentioned in 1937 that Mrs Greville claimed to have paid the former monarch's bill for some dental treatment. She was less keen on the King of Spain, as he did not always behave like a gentleman in her opinion – '…though he was a Hapsburg, one always felt that he had only just *arrived*'.

She was genuinely fond of the Duke and Duchess of York and had planned to leave Polesden Lacey to them as their country house. Beverley Nichols later remarked that 'this was indeed a true friendship … one of the nicest things about Maggie was her unaffected love for the lady who is now the Queen-Mother… She once said to me that if she had ever had a daughter she would have wished her to be like the Queen-Mother.' Certainly, Polesden became a bolt hole for them at times of stress. There are more than 40 meetings with Mrs Greville in the Duke's appointments diary, as well as the many occasions when they were both guests at the same event.

Margaret Greville prided herself on her shrewd ability to spot people who would be successful and who had the commitment to achieve what they set out to do. However, this facet of her character had an inherent flaw – she was also attracted to driven, ambitious individuals like Oswald Mosley, Ribbentrop and Adolf Hitler.

Power and Politics

"She sat back in a large chair, like a Phoenician goddess, while the cabinet minister or ambassador leant forward attentively … I have no doubt that she had considerable influence."

(Kenneth Clark)

Mrs Greville enjoyed proximity to power. She liked the magnetic pull of influence, the intrigues, the deals and the alliances. Astute politicians were aware that in her orbit they could meet the wealthy and well-connected, furthering their own aims. She cultivated her most important guests at Polesden, where Sir Samuel Hoare, Sir John Simon, Sir Robert Vansittart, or ambassadors such as Grandi and Ribbentrop, would be singled out for a 'quiet little chat' in her study after dinner.

Bob Boothby, a promising MP, described Mrs Greville as having 'the shrewdness of a typical lowland Scot'. He said she was 'a bit of an old bag, but very good to me'. Boothby also found her to be honest; she mentioned one evening that Rufus Isaacs, Lord Reading, had visited Polesden to ask her if he should accept the Viceroyalty of India. Early the next morning, sceptical Boothby went down to consult the visitors' book in the entrance hall – there, on the appropriate date, was the single signature 'Reading'.

Left: **Winston Churchill in 1940.**

Hints of romance

Her affection for Rufus Isaacs appears genuine and heartfelt; she had known him since around 1913. She wrote to him in very affectionate terms after her sojourn in India in 1921–22 ('…never, never can I forget all your kindness to me on my visit to you…your ever grateful, devoted and adoring friend, Maggie Greville'). When he was ill with pneumonia early in 1931, she visited him at home; a few months later she became seriously ill with a similar complaint at the Ritz Hotel in Paris, and he demanded daily bulletins on her progress from her private secretary, and British Embassy staff, telegraphing, 'Anxious have news of Mrs Greville. Please give her my best love. Reading'

In 1926 Rufus Isaacs was created a marquis, the first commoner to have risen so high since the Duke of Wellington. Rufus and Maggie maintained a lively, gossipy and affectionate correspondence for much of the 1920s and early 1930s. In January 1930 Lady Reading died. Subsequently, it is possible to read a certain amount of hope in Mrs Greville's letters; but eighteen months later Rufus Isaacs, aged nearly 71, married Stella Charnaud, 37, his former private secretary.

Mrs Greville wrote to congratulate him, saying that Stella '…struck me as a very charming clever woman'. Mrs Greville cultivated both the Readings as friends, though she would occasionally arrange to see him when his wife was away – a typical handwritten note from the early 1930s reads: 'My Dear. Duchess of York is coming to the theatre on Wed. and I said who shall I invite and she said do try and get Lord Reading. I do so hope you can manage it – we will only be 4. Please phone. Affectionately, Maggie.' Their lengthy friendship ended with Rufus Isaacs' death on 30 December 1935.

Sir John Simon, a widower with children, was also romantically linked with Margaret Greville in the late 1920s. A brilliant lawyer, memorably described as 'a snake in snake's clothing', between 1913 and 1945 he held every major office of state except that of Prime Minister, becoming in succession Attorney-General, Home Secretary, Foreign Secretary, Chancellor of the Exchequer and Lord Chancellor.

There are various theories about why Sir John and Margaret Greville did not marry. Some said that he needed a more compliant wife than Mrs Greville if he was to be Prime Minister; she claimed she would have married him had he not had children. Mrs Greville would point to a spot on the carpet and recount that 'Jack Simon fell on his knees to ask me to marry him. I refused.' Leo Amery MP heard that after this rejection, Sir John wrote to Mrs Greville, vowing that he would now marry the first woman available.

Mrs Greville would point to a spot on the carpet and recount that 'Jack Simon fell on his knees to ask me to marry him. I refused.'

The new Lady Simon was not popular in their social circles. As Austen Chamberlain wrote to his sister from Polesden Lacey on 2 January 1932: 'For really desperate, boreing [sic] vulgarity, commend me to Lady S [imon]. She was the first Lady S's nurse. I should think the noise she made killed her patient, and when Maggie after long hesitation finally decided that she would not marry Sir John, off he went in a huff and married this woman forthwith. If I had done the same I should end on the gallows…'

Oswald Mosley claimed, 'She had an intelligence acute enough to attract the diverse allegiance of the ascetic Sir John Simon, and the bucolic Sir Robert Horne. She mixed her company well, and also her dishes.' The

Scottish-born Robert Horne KC was a successful businessman, advocate and MP, and Chancellor of the Exchequer 1921–22. Between 1926 and 1940 he stayed at Polesden 49 times, and lunched or dined at Charles Street on 60 occasions. A suave and well-groomed bachelor, he was described by Stanley Baldwin as 'a womanising cad', but he and Mrs Greville were on the best of terms for many years.

Another favoured guest was Frederick Lindemann, a brilliant scientist, and a teetotal vegetarian, a rarity for his age and circle. A gifted tennis player, he is probably the only professor to have competed at Wimbledon. When the Great War broke out, he researched the new science of aviation. He solved the theoretical problem of how pilots could extricate themselves from a spin, and then learnt to fly in order to demonstrate his theory was correct. Fortunately, he was right, and many lives were saved, including his own. Following the war he became a professor of physics at the University of Oxford. Between July 1926 and August 1939, he was Mrs Greville's guest in London or Surrey on more than 50 occasions. 'The Prof' travelled in a Rolls-Royce, driven by a chauffeur and accompanied by a valet; he enjoyed female company and was an excellent, well-informed gossip.

Relations with leading figures

Mrs Greville had strong views on many of the leading figures of the day, and was not backward in expressing them. Of the Prime Minister Stanley Baldwin, she said, 'Really my dear, one could not possibly be *seen* with Mr Baldwin.' She was an implacable enemy of Lord George Lloyd, whom she had first encountered in India in 1921–2. He had irritated her by fluffing a hand of bridge with disastrous consequences for his partner, the cash-strapped Queen of Spain, under Mrs Greville's roof. She said of him, 'Lord Lloyd had the impertinence to imagine that he was going to be the Viceroy of India, but I soon put a stop to *that*!' Ever vitriolic, she sent him a deprecating telegram when he was appointed to the House of Lords, saying, 'I thought you were ambitious.'

Mrs Greville was initially impressed by the charismatic Oswald Mosley, who was in great demand in many London drawing rooms at the end of the First World War. He was a dashing former Royal Flying Corps officer, still on crutches while he recovered from war injuries. He described her parties as 'sedate', but it was in Charles Street that he met the leading politicians of the day and was taken up by Sir George Younger, Conservative Whip, who was Margaret Greville's relative. Mrs Greville encouraged Mosley's idealistic political ambitions, which in those days were progressive, as were many of the new intake of young Tories, and when he was returned as an MP in December 1923 she sent him a handwritten note:

"Bravo bravo bravo my dear Mr Mosley – I am overjoyed at yr. majority – all my congratulations. Don't answer this you will be snowed up with congratulations but I had to add mine they are so sincere."

Yrs ever, Margaret Greville

The most complex of Mrs Greville's many political relationships, and one that lasted decades, despite friction, was with Winston Churchill. Their families were closely linked; Winston had been a friend and supporter of Ronnie Greville's career as an MP, and the Grevilles and the McEwans were friends of Winston's parents, Lord and Lady Randolph Churchill. In later years she maintained an almost proprietorial interest in Winston, respecting his abilities even when she did not agree with his views, during his 'wilderness years'. Winston and Clementine, as well as their daughter Diana, spent weekends at Polesden, and Mrs Greville was a guest at Diana's wedding in 1932.

In the 1930s Beverley Nichols remembered Winston Churchill holding forth on a number of occasions over the dining table at Polesden Lacey, and was spellbound.

"His 'finest hour' was after dinner, when the ladies had left the table, with more than usually earnest entreaties that we should not be too long over our port, for they knew from bitter experience that when Winston was at a dinner table with a good cigar in one hand and a better Armagnac in the other, the chances were that they would be left without cavaliers until

*nearly bedtime, and would have to spend the rest of the evening hissing
at each other over acres of Aubusson. Even as I write I can see Winston,
tilting back his chair, warming a balloon glass of the precious Armagnac
between his palms…Over this table he delivered some of his most sombre
prophecies, and always, of course, they were about Germany, and always
too he seemed to see Germany as a machine, a sort of steel monster that
was clanking down the corridors of history towards us."*

The ambassadors

*"…old Mrs Ronnie Greville, who used to feel déclassée if there were not at
least two ambassadors in her weekend party…"*

(Beverley Nichols)

As a well-connected opinion-former, Mrs Greville was a frequent guest in the
1920s and 1930s at receptions, soirées and parties held by many London
embassies. In return, she regularly invited ambassadors to dinner in Charles
Street, or to stay for the weekend – or even longer – at Polesden Lacey. They
made arrangements for her to visit their respective countries, providing every
benefit, from the use of private trains and dedicated interpreters, to arranging
meetings with their heads of state.

The particular vision of Britain she offered must have been seductive.
A summer weekend spent at luxurious Polesden Lacey appealed to the
representatives of many strife-ridden countries. Similarly, to be invited for
Christmas to this country house, unusually well heated and run like the very
best hotel, was balm to the homesick diplomatic soul. Unsurprisingly, Mrs
Greville and her ambassadors found much to admire in each other.

*Tea is at 5 o'clock, and not 5 minutes past…which means that the Spanish
Ambassador who has gone for a walk down the yew avenue, hastily
retraces his steps, and the Chancellor of the Exchequer…hurries down the
great staircase, and the various gentlemen rise from their chaise-longues
and join the procession to the tea room…*

(Beverley Nichols, All I Could Never Be)

Margaret Greville was fond of Leopold von Hoesch, the German Ambassador. Suave and congenial, he disliked National Socialism, but was obliged to represent his country's interests after Adolf Hitler came to power in January 1933. Mrs Greville was also friendly with Prince and Princess Otto von Bismarck; he was *chargé d'affairs* at the German Embassy in the early 1930s, and their names appear as guests at both her houses, for meals and for weekend visits, in her records between 1930 and 1937.

Perhaps the most charming ambassador she knew was Count Dino Grandi, an early supporter of Mussolini in the 1920s, who was rewarded with a prominent diplomatic career. In 1932 he arrived in London as the Italian Ambassador. Sociable and handsome, Grandi told people exactly what they wanted to hear, while gently promoting the cause of Fascism, Italian style. Mrs Greville visited Italy shortly after Mussolini had taken power and had had a 'long talk' with him, as well as an audience with the Pope. Grandi was genuinely dismayed by the deterioration of relations between Italy and Britain, due to Mussolini's increasing closeness to Germany, and he assured Mrs Greville that his only desire was for peace.

Above: **Mrs Greville was an *Ehrengast*, a 'guest of honour' of the Third Reich, and attended the Nuremberg Rally in 1934. 'I have returned full of amazement…I adored my visit', she wrote.**

Her most controversial diplomatic relationship, however, was with the German Ambassador, Ribbentrop, which was to bring her considerable censure. Robert Bruce Lockhart was sure that she was misled by Ribbentrop, who cultivated her from their very first meeting. It was a relationship that started with mutual appreciation, and appears to have ended sourly; as soon as the Ribbentrops returned to Berlin in 1937, Mrs Greville had almost nothing further to do with Germany.

Mrs Greville and Nazi Germany

After the accession of Hitler in January 1933, Mrs Greville had been one of many people curious to visit Nazi Germany. In late summer 1933 she made a private trip, spending 17 days touring the country. As in former years, she went to Baden-Baden, that familiar haunt of Edwardians in need of a 'cure', but she also visited the medieval cities of Nuremberg and Rothenburg, Stuttgart, Dresden, Berlin and Cologne. Meanwhile, von Hoesch had recommended to the new regime that they should offer familiarisation trips to certain British opinion formers. As a result, Mrs Greville received an invitation to attend the 1934 Nuremberg Rally, in the name of the Führer, authorised by his deputy, Rudolf Hess.

This vast spectacle of National Socialist ideology and military might was a showcase for Hitler. Overseas visitors of influence were known as '*Ehrengast*', 'Guests of Honour'. They were met on arrival by personal aides de camp, accompanied to their luxury hotels, provided with assistance, interpreters and drivers, taken to soirées, receptions and parties, and shown selected aspects of the New Germany.

The Daily Mail on 11 September 1934 reported that, among the many foreign visitors in Nuremberg for the 'Partei-Tag' was Mrs Ronald Greville, who was staying in the Grand Hotel and who claimed not to have slept since her arrival 48 hours before, so interesting was she finding the atmosphere. On Mrs Greville's return to London, according to Bruce Lockhart, she was 'a convinced pro-German' and 'full of enthusiasm for Hitler'. She complained that no one from the British Embassy in Berlin went to this event – after all, the British Ambassador in Moscow turned out for Communist celebrations on 1 May and 7 November in Red Square. In a handwritten letter to her friend 'Prof.' Lindemann, she wrote: '...I hear you were in Germany. So was I for 17 days and I have returned full of amazement...I adored my visit...'

"That brilliant powerful personality Mrs Ronald Greville is back. She was entertained by Hitler at the Nuremberg festivities last month, and is now enthusiastic over 'the little brown shirts.'"

(Tatler, *24 October 1934*)

Hitler was wary of contact with anyone outside his immediate social and political circle. However, this tenacious British widow managed to obtain an audience with him. On 12 September 1934 Sir Eric Phipps, British Ambassador to Berlin, sent a report to George V:

Below: **Invitation sent to Mrs Greville in the name of the Fuhrer, issued by Rudolf Hess, to attend the Nuremberg Rally of 1934.**

Der Führer
beehrt sich, Sie zum
Reichsparteitag der N.S.D.A.P.,
welcher vom 5.–10. September 1934 in Nürnberg stattfindet, einzuladen.
Ich bitte Sie, bis zum 27. August 1934 um Mitteilung auf
beiliegender Karte, ob Sie der Einladung folgen.
In diesem Falle werden Ihnen die Ehren-
karten, Programm und Unterkunfts-
bescheinigung zugeleitet.
Mit deutschem Gruß
gez. R. Heß

"Baron von Neurath ... told me that he had seen Mrs Ronald Greville at Nuremberg, where she had been invited as a guest of the German government. Mrs Greville had expressed a wish to be received by the Fuhrer and although it had been difficult he [Baron von Neurath] had been able to arrange for a short meeting of a few minutes. Mrs Greville was, it seems, delighted."

Any records regarding Hitler and the Nazis were almost certainly among the personal papers destroyed by Bole after Mrs Greville's death in 1942. Given her lifelong enthusiasm for 'collecting' dukes and dictators, maharajahs and millionaires, it is likely that she would have used Hitler's name until it no longer suited her purposes. However, as a valued 'Guest of the Reich' she also saw him at rallies and events, spot-lit and ranting, surrounded by thousands, and may have been taken in, as others were by his hypnotic powers.

Kenneth Clark described Mrs G as the queen of a pro-Nazi circle 'who closed their eyes to Hitler because they, mistakenly, supposed that the Nazis were less likely to take away their money than the Bolshies.'

Back in London, following the suspiciously convenient death of Ambassador von Hoesch in April 1936, Ribbentrop took on the role of ambassador. He issued invitations to many influential Britons to attend the Berlin Olympics, including Mrs Greville. She travelled to Germany to attend the Games, but was taken ill at Baden-Baden some days before and was forced to recuperate in the spa town, so she missed them.

Mrs Greville continued to entertain German VIPs, such as Prince Philip of Hesse, a close personal friend of Goering, a supporter of Hitler and President of Prussia; between 1934 and 1937 he dined at Charles Street three times. The general pro-German attitude to be found at Mrs Greville's table repelled some of her other guests. Harold Nicolson, lunching at Charles Street in June 1936, vividly recalled a clash of ideologies:

"I sat next to a German woman who tried a little Nazi propaganda. Poor wretch, she did not know that she had a tiger lurking beside her.

*'Do you know my country, sir?' she asked. 'Yes, I have often visited
Germany.' 'Have you been there recently, since our movement?' 'No,
except for an hour at Munich, I have not visited Germany since 1930.'
'Oh, but you should come now, you would find it all so changed.'
'Yes, I should find all my old friends either in prison, or exiled,
or murdered.' At which she gasped like a fish."*

In the summer of 1937 Mrs Greville began dropping her contacts with
the German Embassy. She held a glorious dinner party on 23 June 1937 in
Charles Street, inviting many important guests. The Brazilian Ambassador
and his wife, great friends of Maggie and frequent houseguests at Polesden,
were there, along with a contingent from the Japanese Embassy, but Frau
Ribbentrop attended alone, as her husband had been recalled to Berlin for
a meeting.

Mrs Greville made a final visit to Germany in August
1937, which coincided with Ribbentrop's final return to
Berlin. He was appointed Foreign Minister the following
year. His successor as Ambassador to London, Herbert
von Dirksen, does not appear in any of Mrs Greville's
guest lists.

**Through her association
with Nazi Germany, Mrs
Greville's reputation had
been damaged.**

For many former friends of Germany, 'Kristallnacht' in November 1938
was the final straw; the wholesale destruction of synagogues and the seizure
of Jewish businesses and the murder or internment of their owners left little
room for doubt about the true nature of the regime.

Through her association with Nazi Germany, Mrs Greville's reputation had
been damaged. As Bruce Lockhart remarked, 'No-one doubted her
patriotism; it was her judgment they questioned.' In July 1937 Harold
Nicolson had attended a luncheon party given by the novelist Mary Borden,
and was dismayed to find himself seated next to Mrs Greville. The gloves
were off: 'How comes it that this plump but virulent little bitch should hold
such social power?' he wrote later to his wife. He was also concerned about
the misinformation spread by society hostesses to the representatives of
fascist dictatorships; he wrote in his diary in April 1939:

"I do not believe that any intelligent man such as Grandi could have left him [Mussolini] under any illusion that the will-power of this country is concentrated in Mrs Ronald Greville. He must know that in the last resort our decision is embodied, not in Mayfair or Cliveden, but in the provinces. The harm which these silly, selfish hostesses do is really immense. They convey to foreign envoys the impression that policy is decided in their own drawing-rooms...these people have a subversive influence."

Anti-Semitism in Britain in the 1930s

As was rapidly becoming clear, central to Nazi ideology was the persecution of the Jews, but Germany was far from being the only nation to discriminate against this particular religion. Anti-Semitism existed throughout Europe, including, of course, Britain.

Below: **Mrs Greville with Baron Golschem Rothschild.**

Some commentators have accused Margaret Greville of anti-Semitism. It is true that she had strong likes and dislikes, but she tended to take individuals as she found them. She appreciated and promoted talent, and employed Jewish people, such as Mewès and Davis, on two major projects that were important to her – the refurbishment of both her homes. She was also romantically attached to Rufus Isaacs, Lord Reading, an observant Jew. She greatly respected Sir Ernest Cassel, Edward VII's astute financial adviser, and was protective towards his granddaughter, Edwina Ashley, who was half-Jewish. She furthered the cause of the politician Leslie Hore-Belisha, whose first name was Isaac.

In addition, she was friendly with various members of the Rothschild family, as well as Sir Philip Sassoon. It is notable that among her many friends were successful, wealthy and well-connected people who were Jewish. In this, she

had much in common with the majority of her class and background, who mixed with Jewish people in society, so long as they appeared to integrate with the dominant culture.

There are no traces of Mrs Greville belonging to any organisation that promoted anti-Semitism. Her early enthusiasm for Oswald Mosley quickly petered out as his views became more right-wing, and she welcomed the whole spectrum of political views, preferring intelligent personalities to pernicious ideologies. However, in the 1930s she did make increasingly harsh observations about Jewish people, and in this respect she reflected the attitudes of her time. In one letter to Professor Lindemann, written on her return to Britain from the Nuremberg Rally in October 1934, she notes that as a result of the Nazis coming to power in Germany, '...I do pray and hope that we shan't have an influx of Jews here –I love about five and abhor collectively...', a view that was unfortunately prevalent throughout much of Western society before the Second World War.

There are no traces of Mrs Greville belonging to any organisation that promoted anti-Semitism.

As conflict with Germany loomed, some were convinced that international Jewry was trying to drag Britain into war with Germany. In one particularly vitriolic letter, sent to the author Mary Borden, Margaret Greville wrote:

"I detest persecution, but I regard the Jews as the greatest menace to civilisation at the present moment...their hatred of Hitler is so great (which one can quite understand) that they would not mind if the whole world were plunged into war and civilisation ended if they thought that, by these means, they could finish Hitler..."

Such views seem abhorrent and unthinkable today, in the wake of what is now known about the Holocaust. However, in the 1930s, what was being planned behind closed doors in the New Germany would have seemed totally incredible and repugnant to the power brokers and society hostesses of every civilised country.

Abdication and the Slide to War

"Maggie darling, do tell me about this Mrs Simpson – I have only just heard of her."

(Margaret Greville's account of Emerald Cunard's comment on the Abdication)

During the mid-1930s many Britons seemed preoccupied with national rather than international concerns, absorbed by events at home that threatened to overturn the old order. The crisis was brought about by the passion of the Prince of Wales for Wallis Simpson, a chic, slim American living in London with her second husband, Ernest. On inheriting the throne early in 1936, the Prince was determined to make Wallis his queen, a decision that caused a constitutional crisis. Needless to say, Margaret Greville, being so close to many of the main protagonists, had a front row seat for the Abdication, and its aftermath.

Sir John Simon, then Home Secretary, described the Prince of Wales as 'the man born to be king...the most widely known and universally popular personality in the world', but those who knew him better harboured misgivings. One of the first to express those, unsurprisingly, was Mrs Greville. Her extensive tour of India in 1921–22 coincided with that of the reluctant Prince, and despite her close friendship with his parents, she liked him less after their proximity. She confided these thoughts in a letter to Lord Reading, the Viceroy who had hosted 'HRH', the Prince of Wales, on 27 July 1922:

"...HRH is full of praise for all you did for him ...but HRH is wearing his nerves out in a fruitless life and it is altogether very sad and as F.E. [Smith] said last night he cannot maintain his popularity under existing circumstances..."

She was not alone in her criticisms. In 1927 the Prince's assistant private secretary, Alan 'Tommy' Lascelles, confided in Prime Minister Baldwin that he sometimes thought, while watching the future king competing in a point-to-point, that a broken neck might best benefit the country. Baldwin agreed.

The Prince made the acquaintance of Mr and Mrs Simpson in 1934 and as the relationship developed, Ernest increasingly made his excuses and left the field open. Mrs Simpson became a recognisable figure in London society, where the Prince of Wales's relationship with this smart American was seen as the latest of his habitual dalliances. In the case of Wallis, what began as a perfectly innocent if flattering friendship gathered momentum and became unstoppable.

Opposite: **The marriage of the Duke of Windsor and Wallis Simpson, 3 June 1937.**

Mrs Greville and the Prince of Wales

By the time the Prince was involved with Wallis Simpson, he had little to do with Mrs Greville. He had been an occasional guest at her parties in the 1920s, but the relationship deteriorated. He may have known that Mrs Greville had arranged to leave Polesden Lacey to his younger brother Bertie, rather than to him, when she died. Nevertheless their social circles inevitably overlapped; in June 1933, for example, Margaret's beloved goddaughter Sonia, now Mrs Roland Cubitt, held a cocktail party at her place in Hyde Park Gardens. *Harper's Bazaar* noted that Mrs Cubitt, when entertaining, '…often has the assistance of her godmother, the Hon. Mrs Ronald Greville'. On this occasion, Mrs Greville helped Sonia welcome the Prince of Wales, the Duke and Duchess of York and Prince George, later to become the Duke of Kent. For society hostesses of the time, this was the equivalent of getting three cherries in a row.

Wallis's holiday in Kitzbühel with the Prince of Wales in February 1935 changed her status. Suddenly Wallis and Ernest were cultivated by society hostesses, anxious to attract the Prince of Wales to their tables. However, Wallis incurred the dislike of the Duchess of York, in the spring of 1935, when she was overheard by Elizabeth imitating her to a sycophantic group of guests at the Prince's home. Battlelines were drawn, and Mrs Greville was aware that the Prince's unsuitable 'friend' would not be welcome in the very smartest drawing rooms.

> *Suddenly Wallis and Ernest were cultivated by society hostesses, anxious to also attract the Prince of Wales to their tables.*

In August 1935 Hugh Lloyd Thomas, a friend of the Prince of Wales, stated that the Prince 'will not have Mrs Greville in his house or go to hers', which was a statement terse to the point of rudeness in such circles. Intriguingly, 'Chips' Channon's invaluable diary contains a clue; his entry for 14 May 1935 relates a schism occurring in London society between Mrs Simpson, nominally the gatekeeper to York House, the Prince's home, and an influential but unnamed hostess:

"There is tremendous excitement about Mrs Simpson, who has now banned --- and all her group from York House. It is war to the knife between the past and the present. Officially I am on ---'s side but secretly

delighted, for she was always an appallingly selfish, silly influence.
Mrs Simpson has enormously improved the Prince. In fact I find the
duel over the Prince of Wales between Mrs Simpson, supported by
Diana Cooper and, strangely enough, Emerald, and the --- camp is
most diverting..."

It is hard to think of another candidate whose name could fill the blanks as well as Mrs Greville's. She was a useful acquaintance of Chips, though his views on her were mixed. Diana Cooper constantly irritated Mrs Greville, who in 1931 attempted to sabotage the Parliamentary career of Diana's husband, Duff. Meanwhile, Emerald Cunard had facilitated the budding romance with her intimate little dinners. Suddenly, there was the 'old guard' and the 'new circle'. The Yorks were not invited to Emerald's dinner parties, scintillating with wit and repartee, or to Lady Sibyl Colefax's intellectual lunches, but they gravitated to the more traditional crowd around Mrs Greville: the statesmen, ambassadors, millionaires and foreign royalty.

In May 1935, the country celebrated the Silver Jubilee of King George V and Queen Mary. The Prince of Wales had insisted to his father that his 'friend' Wallis Simpson should attend the Silver Jubilee Court Ball, and denied categorically that he was having an affair with her. The King and Queen watched stony-faced as the Prince foxtrotted past with a bony American in green and purple lamé. The Duchess of York, who had previously enjoyed many dances with the Prince herself, was annoyed to be so upstaged. It is likely both the royal ladies discussed their concerns about Wallis with their great friend, Mrs Greville, also in attendance.

1936 – the year of three kings

A mere eight months after he and Queen Mary had marked their Silver Jubilee with great national celebrations, King George V died at Sandringham in January 1936. Queen Mary, mindful of the protocol, kissed the hand of her eldest son, now Edward VIII. He was appalled; his father's death meant the curtailment of his playboy years.

The old King had worried about the succession, and his son's relationship with 'that woman'. He had predicted that, after his death, his oldest son would ruin himself within twelve months, and had hoped that 'David' would never marry and have children, so that Bertie and then 'Lilibet' might inherit the throne.

George V's body was transported from Sandringham to lie in state in Westminster. The day of the funeral at Windsor was bitterly cold. It was a funeral for a family member, but also the last rites afforded to a king; therefore, the Prime Minister Mr Baldwin, and the representatives of Austria, The Netherlands, France, Poland, Germany and Italy all attended.

Below: The abdication crisis of King Edward VIII and Mrs Wallis Simpson reported in *Daily Sketch*, 8 December 1936.

Friends of the family were also present; 'The Hon. Mrs Ronald Greville, who has long been honoured by the late King and Queen Mary, was sitting next to Sir Philip Sassoon', reported the *Sunday Times*. Margaret Greville wrote a letter of condolence to Queen Mary on 7 February 1936, as she was leaving for a trip to Japan: 'I feel I must write and say how much Your Majesty is and will be in my thoughts … I cannot tell or write what I felt at St George's [Chapel] and the quite marvellous fortitude and dignity of Your Majesty. Millions shared your grief and all gave their love and sympathy … I do hope that knowledge has in some manner softened the grief and terrible void...'

The Coronation of the future Edward VIII was planned for 1937. The 'new court' joked about official mourning, with Wallis claiming that she hadn't worn black stockings since she gave up the Can-Can. Meanwhile, the new 'Edwardians' avoided the old 'Georgians', senior hostesses such as Mrs Greville with her heavyweight

politicians and power brokers, and Edward's brother and sister-in-law, the rather more homely Yorks. 'The idea of Bertie and Elizabeth having a "set" made us all laugh,' said Lady Cunard.

Later in 1936 Wallis's name discreetly appeared at the divorce courts in provincial Ipswich, and in November the Prince of Wales informed Prime Minister Stanley Baldwin that he intended to marry Wallis. The British press had so far suppressed all stories about the King's affair, but overseas, press speculation was rife. What the American journalist H.L. Mencken described as 'The Greatest Story since the Crucifixion' featured regularly in foreign papers and magazines. Some Britons were puzzled to receive their overseas magazines with features snipped out. Those in the know had mixed feelings; 'Why should the King not have his cutie?' mused Winston Churchill. 'Because the British people do not want a Queen Cutie,' snapped Noël Coward.

The matter came to a head when the press finally had a spurious excuse to break into print. On 1 December 1936 the Bishop of Bradford, whose surname was Blunt, made a vague allusion to the King's 'need for grace', meaning his infrequent attendances at church. The so-called 'Blunt Instrument' fractured the wall of silence. By 2 December, the story was appearing in provincial papers. Wallis Simpson, whose windows had been broken by bricks, left for the Continent the same day. On the morning of 3 December newspaper placards boomed 'The King's Marriage', reporting the constitutional crisis, that Edward, being head of the Church of England, could not divorce and re-marry if his ex-spouse was still alive, so he could not marry Wallis Simpson and remain on the throne. The secret was out.

> *The British press had so far suppressed all stories about the King's affair, but overseas, press speculation was rife.*

The Abdication

It was a dreadful week for the House of Windsor. On 10 December
the uncrowned King let it be known that he was abdicating, and it was
announced to the House of Commons by Baldwin on 11 December.
That evening the Royal Family dined together at Fort Belvedere, an unhappy
occasion for all involved. On 12 December 1936 Edward VIII broadcast to
the nation, announcing he was relinquishing the crown in order to marry
'the woman I love'. Significantly, he praised his younger brother and
mentioned his 'matchless blessing not bestowed to me – a happy house
and his wife and children'.

The Duke and Duchess of York suddenly found themselves to be the next
King and Queen; Edward VIII having deserted his post, as they saw it,
they had no choice but to accept. Bertie found public speaking traumatic;
he had a bad stammer, and strong emotions made his problems worse. Now
he would have to take on a public role for which he had not been prepared.
His father was dead, his mother was shocked to the core by events and his

Left: **The Duke and
Duchess of York, with
Princess Elizabeth and
Princess Margaret Rose,
in 1935.**

elder brother had damaged the whole edifice on which the monarchy was based and escaped to be with 'that woman', apparently without a backward glance. Elizabeth was livid; her original doubts about marrying Bertie had been because she did not want to join the Royal Family, and now she was thrust into the limelight. She took to her bed at 145, Piccadilly with influenza, and stayed there till the constitutional maelstrom passed. She subsequently blamed the Windsors for her beloved husband's early death.

Elizabeth was livid; her original doubts about marrying Bertie had been because she did not want to join the Royal Family, and now she was thrust into the limelight.

Margaret Greville wrote in encouragement to the new King on the day that Edward VIII's Abdication speech was broadcast:

"I have had my thoughts concentrated upon a truly happy family these last terrible days of anxiety, but knowing that thousands of letters would be arriving I felt it would be an intrusion to add to the pile, but I can no longer resist. We all acclaim Your Majesty … I feel a special joy as I know so well your greatness, modesty, unswerving sense of duty and everything that represents the best in English life. I know that I will not have the same privilege of seeing you as before Sir but I will always stand aside and rejoice in your success and the beloved consort she who radiates peace and happiness.

I have the honour to remain, with deepest devotion, Your Majesty's humble, obedient subject, Margaret Greville."

The new King and Queen, with a Coronation set for 12 May 1937, needed help and support. Osbert Sitwell was a friend of Elizabeth, having met her at Mrs Greville's weekend parties at Polesden Lacey. He wrote a scathing poem called 'Rat Week', in which he attacked those false 'friends' of the King who had courted him and Mrs Simpson until their loss of status, at which point they deserted them. This was circulated privately – Mrs Greville was one of those who received a copy, as was Elizabeth.

Mrs Greville's engagement book for guests at Charles Street between 6 and 13 December 1936 is unprecedentedly packed with names. One of them, on 10 December, was Lady Cunard, who had last graced the household in

July 1935, 18 months before. This was Mrs Greville's opportunity to score against Emerald; afterwards she claimed all over London that her rival said, 'Maggie darling, *do* tell me about this Mrs Simpson – I have only just heard of her!'

Mrs Greville retired to Polesden for Christmas, and at her first weekend house party of 1937, the guests included Prince and Princess Bismarck, the Belgian and Chilean Ambassadors, the Sacheverell Sitwells and Beverley Nichols. With such an avid audience and a gripping news story, the well-connected Mrs Greville was in her element.

In February 1937, the new King and Queen and their two little girls moved into Buckingham Palace.

In February 1937 the new King and Queen and their two little girls moved into Buckingham Palace. The marriage of the former king and the now single Wallis was scheduled for early summer, and the King, taking advice from Sir John Simon, wrote to his brother to say that no member of their family would attend the ceremony. Queen Elizabeth and Queen Mary thwarted David's attempt to obtain the title of 'Her Royal Highness' for Wallis. In fact, the wife of an abdicated king who had the title HRH was also entitled to bear it, though any children would not – but the Duchess of Windsor could expect no more. The new Queen's animosity for Wallis was implacable.

If any further proof were needed as to Margaret Greville's allegiances, *The Daily Mail* in May 1937 had to issue a prominent correction, stating that it had been 'erroneously reported' that the Hon. Mrs Greville had visited the Chateau de Candé near Tours in France. The chateau was where the Duke of Windsor had finally been reunited with Wallis Simpson, as they made preparations for their marriage. Osbert Sitwell, in a letter to Elizabeth, wrote: 'You can imagine how furious poor Mrs Ronnie, at the moment in Paris, will be when she hears of it, and what thunderbolts will fall on the heads of the editors of the Daily Mail...' 'Time was when any mistake of that kind would have been overlooked,' reported the *New York Times*, gleefully.

The New Court

No one could have anticipated that the dutiful and domesticated Duke and Duchess of York, such friends of Mrs Greville, that great collector of royalty, would become King and Queen. 'I was so happy in the days when they used to run in and out of my house as if they were my children…' she said, as though she was their favourite aunt. Significantly, she kept an unattributed newspaper clipping from 3 July 1937, which states:

"…Mrs Greville was 'the friend' who gave the then Duchess of York the beautiful triple rope of pearls which she wears so constantly.

There are people who say, too, the Princess Margaret Rose's name was chosen as a compliment to this very dear friend of her parents."

It is most likely that Mrs Greville herself was the source of this story; her star was in the ascendant since the Abdication, and she was '*amie de la maison*' at Buckingham Palace.

In return, Mrs Greville's cosy relationship with the media was occasionally useful for the Royal Family, to plant stories in the press. After the Abdication, the former Edward VIII had implied that in relinquishing the throne he would suffer financially. This was untrue; as the Prince of Wales he had enjoyed an income of £100,000 a year from the Duchy of Cornwall for a number of years. He had never run an expensive household, and his later economies in sacking staff were in fact to fund extravagant gifts for Wallis, as well as paying her maintenance.

The Duke spread the impression, especially to his friends in the United States, that he had been mistreated by the Royal Family and left very hard up because of his love for American-born Wallis. On 8 March 1937 a damning letter appeared in the influential *Time* magazine, written by A.E.L. Bennett, who claimed to be an American living in Paris. He said:

"At least 95% of the British Empire are utterly disgusted with Edward VIII…he dismissed hundreds of employees at Balmoral & Sandringham, and sold off everything on these properties which was saleable, and with the money thus saved and raised, he bought priceless emeralds for Mrs Simpson. These emeralds were the

property of Queen Alexandra who left them to Princess Victoria, who in turn sold them to Garrard's of Bond Street, where King Edward bought them…"

This robust account effectively scotched any suggestion that the former Prince might have been left poverty-stricken. Mr Bennett mentioned in the published letter that 'these stones are very large and magnificent, but have many flaws. The lady who gave me this information is a personal friend of Queen Mary and the Royal Family, but I cannot tell you her name.' Bizarrely and probably published in error, immediately below this statement appears the following paragraph:

May I suggest to you that the lady who will be very much in the eye of society, if not the public, will be the Hon. Mrs. Ronald Greville, a very rich lady, who has always been very much with the new King & Queen (indeed their honeymoon was spent at Polesden Lacey, her country house) and who is supposed to have named the Queen as her eventual heiress.

Needless to say, a copy of the page from *Time* magazine appears in the Polesden Lacey press clippings book, compiled by Mrs Greville's cuttings agency in the 1930s.

The Coronation of 1937

The Queen was very conscious that 1936 had been 'the year of three kings', and the Abdication had unsettled the monolithic image of the British monarchy. The public had been let down by the heir; now they were coming to terms with the 'spare'. Doubts had been expressed as to whether 'poor old Bertie' was up to the job; rigorous practice and speech therapy gave him confidence in public speaking. The Queen needed a suitably regal image, so the couturier Norman Hartnell devised a highly feminine style for her, recalling nineteenth-century princesses. The contrast in image between the soft-focus Queen Elizabeth and the hard-edged Duchess of Windsor was unmistakable.

Doubts had been expressed as to whether 'poor old Bertie' was up to the job; rigorous practice and speech therapy gave him confidence in public speaking.

Right: **King George VI and Queen Elizabeth with their daughters Princess Elizabeth (later Queen Elizabeth II) and Princess Margaret Rose in coronation robes.**

George R.I.
1937

Elizabeth R

The new King and Queen had remembered their old friend; in March 1937 the King had a letter sent to Mrs Greville inviting her to have a prestigious seat in the royal box for the Coronation. Osbert Sitwell planned to stay at Charles Street the night before the ceremony, as he was escorting Mrs Greville to the Abbey. Recalling lively weekends they had both spent at Polesden Lacey, he wrote to Elizabeth that he feared, 'I shall have to depend on Bole and Bacon and the "Crazy Week Gang" to help me dress in the morning! Goodness knows what they may not make of such an occasion! I imagine they have already been celebrating the Coronation…'

On 12 May 1937 – Coronation Day – thousands thronged the streets of London to cheer while the King and Queen drove in the State Coach from Buckingham Palace to Westminster Abbey. The new monarchs were profoundly glad to get through the ordeal, but for the rest of London it was an opportunity for celebration. The Channons threw a dinner party: their guests included a 'brace of princelings, Ernst August of Hanover, and Fritzy of Prussia' (the grandson of the Kaiser), and Mrs Greville was delighted to be seated next to him. After dinner the party set off to the Duke and Duchess of Sutherland's ball, where the new King and Queen and Queen Mary welcomed their guests. Mrs Greville responded in kind, putting on a 'stupendous' dinner party at Charles Street on 24 May. Forty guests were introduced to King Farouk of Egypt and his mother, Queen Nazli.

Though inevitably their duties now took up far more of their time, Margaret Greville was among the guests at the King and Queen's first dinner party at Buckingham Palace following their accession. They dined at Charles Street at the end of June 1937, and they regularly exchanged affectionate letters. In September 1937 Mrs Greville sent the Queen a joke she had heard about the fashion for 'Wallis Hats', so-called because they had 'no crown'.

Ill-health, and the slide to war

By Christmas 1937 Mrs Greville was spending increasing amounts of time in a wheelchair, as she had difficulty in walking, but she still held court at Polesden Lacey. After 19 weeks of illness she was able to travel to Monte Carlo to convalesce, but her health was giving cause for concern. At least she had company: Osbert Sitwell, who had been diagnosed as suffering from gout, spent a fortnight with her at Monte Carlo, and he described their days as a 'sort of Bath-chair race'. He wrote to the Queen on 20 March 1938, that 'Mrs Ronnie is much better though she still can't walk, and was quite at her best...for an invalid, she is wonderfully gay; and sent for several Germans from San Remo in order to tell them what she thought of their behaviour...'

It took till the end of May 1938 for Mrs Greville to resume her social life. In June the King and Queen invited her to use the Royal Entrance at Ascot so that she didn't have to walk far. Shortly afterwards she had a serious attack of phlebitis and a consultant was flown from Vienna to treat her. For most of the summer and autumn of 1938 she was seriously ill and confined to Charles Street.

Beverley Nichols recalled that Mrs Greville burst into tears, the only time he had ever seen her cry, and exclaimed, 'Oh, my dear Twenty-five, what it would be to have a daughter like that!'

In June 1938 Lady Strathmore, the mother of Queen Elizabeth, died after a long illness at the age of 75. The King and Queen were preparing for a State visit to France in July, and Norman Hartnell remade the Queen's entire wardrobe in white, the regal alternative for mourning. Her dresses were a sensation, accompanied by diamonds and pearls borrowed from the Royal Family's holdings. The visit was a triumph, improving the *entente cordiale*.

On the day they returned to London, the Queen, having heard that Margaret Greville was ill in bed, visited Charles Street and sat by her bedside to tell her all about their visit. Beverley Nichols recalled that Mrs Greville burst into tears, the only time he had ever seen her cry, and exclaimed, 'Oh, my dear Twenty-five, what it would be to have a daughter like that!' After which, ashamed of her display of emotion – for it was her policy to emphasise her worldliness – she sat up abruptly and ordered half a bottle of champagne, and was very rude to the footman who brought it.

Christmas 1938 Mrs Greville spent at Polesden Lacey with a smaller than usual house party, and although her condition improved she now used a wheelchair frequently. In January 1939 she went to a birthday lunch at Claridge's held in honour of the American millionaire Myron Taylor, and the King and Queen had a quiet dinner with her at Charles Street in February to wish her 'bon voyage' for her trip to Monte Carlo to convalesce. The rail journey was arduous; a special ramp had been made to allow her wheelchair access to the carriage. However, on her arrival in Monte Carlo she fell ill with pneumonia, which was so serious that she could not return to London till mid-April 1939.

On arrival in Monte Carlo she fell ill with pneumonia, which was so serious that she could not return to London till mid-April 1939.

During that last summer of 1939, on the eve of war, there was a palpable sense of tension. Philip Sassoon, witty and urbane friend of Margaret Greville, fell ill with flu. He was very depressed about the news from Europe and was well aware through his international business connections of the punitive treatment of the Jews in Germany. He announced that 'I shall never get better', and died on 3 June 1939, at the age of only 51.

Mrs Greville's progress was slow, but by mid-summer she was able to attend occasional functions, such as the coming-out party for Rosalind Cubitt, daughter of Sonia, Margaret's goddaughter, on 6 July at Ilchester House. The King and Queen were the guests of honour, and Mrs Greville, wearing the magnificent five-strand diamond necklace, was carried up the stairs in a wheelchair by two of her footmen. The Queen also came to visit her at Charles Street throughout the summer when her other duties permitted. They visited the Royal Naval College, Dartmouth with the two princesses. The Captain's Messenger of the Day was Prince Philip of Greece and

Denmark, whose uncle Lord Louis Mountbatten was also in attendance. Handsome Philip caught the attention of young Princess Elizabeth.

At last Mrs Greville was well enough to go down to Polesden Lacey. She still used a wheelchair but could walk a little. 'Chips' Channon visited her there on 4 August:

"...I drove in the rain to Polesden Lacey where I had not been for 15 years, a long time...When I arrived I was told, grandly, that Mrs Greville would see me at 7:30, so I went for a walk meanwhile and got caught in a shower. I returned dripping but was at once shown up to Maggie's little boudoir. I found her changed, older, and thinner. Her hair is quite grey. We gossiped, and she proceeded to be awful about Mrs Vanderbilt whom she hates. There is no one on earth quite so skilfully malicious as old Maggie. She told me that Mrs Vanderbilt had said that she wanted to live in England. 'No, Grace, we have enough Queens here already,' Maggie had retorted. She was vituperative about almost everyone, for about 40 minutes, and it was a scramble to get dressed..."

Mrs Greville had intended to go to France at the end of August 1939, but her travel plans were overtaken by events. Amid rising tension in Europe, culminating in the German invasion of Poland, she stayed at Polesden Lacey. Over the weekend of 2–3 September, she had two of her favourite male friends as house guests, Henry Harris and Sir Robert Horne.

At 11.15 on the Sunday morning, Prime Minster Neville Chamberlain, the architect of the Munich agreement, broadcast on the radio. He announced that the British government had waited in vain for a response from Berlin to the British ultimatum, and '...consequently, this country is at war with Germany.'

The Blitz and The Dorchester

"...at least you would be bombed with the right sort of people..."

(Ed Murrow, American war correspondent, on London hotels during the Blitz)

The reality of war was brought home to Polesden Lacey on the first day of the hostilities. After dark on 3 September 30 evacuated children from London arrived unexpectedly, and Mrs Greville had them put up in the staff accommodation above the garages. Most of the menservants had already joined up, and Mr Bole, the Head Steward, was in hospital having an operation, but the remaining staff coped admirably.

In the first weeks of war, large numbers of Mrs Greville's pictures and portable treasures from Charles Street were packed up and sent to the country for safety. Although she closed up her London house for entertaining, she made it available for a committee of diplomatic wives, the League of Diplomatic Seamstresses, who met there to make supplies for the Red Cross, a blameless way for them to undertake useful but apolitical war work.

Mobility problems continued to dog her; she walked short distances with two sticks, but mostly used a wheelchair, which was pushed by her footman. It is evident that the combination of her prolonged ill-health and the onset of war depressed her greatly. In a letter written on 27 December 1939 to her friend Leo Amery, she complained that she had been ill for two years, and had spent a great deal of time in bed, only getting up for dinner.

Pragmatic as ever, Mrs Greville started to make arrangements for her own care in the event of further prolonged illness. She was now 76 years old, although she always claimed to be younger. She therefore wrote a simple document outlining the medical care that she wanted if she was incapacitated, dictating that any nurse assigned to her care should not come near her unless expressly requested. She explained, 'The nurses who attended my Father were always very kind but he hated the sight of them and I was always there to protect him and he died without their presence.'

Early days of war

It was impossible to remain untouched by the war, and Mrs Greville's friends, family and foes were no exception. The safety of Queen Mary was a constant worry to the government, who feared she might be taken hostage in the event of an invasion, so in October 1939 she was unwillingly billeted at Badminton, the home of her niece. Queen Mary had a tendency to impound perfectly serviceable pieces of agricultural machinery on the grounds that they

Opposite: **The Dorchester Hotel, in exclusive Park Lane, London, in the 1930s.**

should be donated to the war's scrap metal fund. Her servants, unhappy at being far from Windsor, kept three suitcases packed at all times, with a fourth to be filled with tiaras and other jewels, in case of evacuation.

Queen Mary was keen to give lifts to hitch-hiking servicemen encountered on the road – one can only imagine the delight of a thumb-wielding, kitbag carrying Tommy turning to incredulity when the posh car stopping for him was found to have Queen Mary on the back seat. As the war progressed, urgent supplies of hock had to be found for the Queen, who drank at least half a bottle every day and had no intention of changing her ways.

Mrs Greville's rivals and the war

Two of Mrs Greville's rival hostesses were determined to tough it out in London; indeed, Emerald Cunard returned to Britain from America before the start of the Blitz. In January 1940, 'Chips' Channon reported that Emerald had sold many of her belongings and left her home in Grosvenor Square, where she had held court for so long. Emerald squeezed herself into a suite at the Dorchester.

Lady Sibyl Colefax had been living in reduced circumstances since the death in 1936 of her husband, Arthur. She threw herself into war work, running a canteen in Belgrave Square, and also organised regular weekly dinners called 'ordinaries' at the Dorchester Hotel, where guests would subsequently be sent a bill for their share of the food and wine. The 'ordinaries' started in September 1941, and as the war progressed, rationing reduced the victuals and increased the cost from 10 shillings a head to 15 shillings, but so stimulating and enjoyable was the company that no one minded paying.

A patriotic gesture

Mrs Greville was aware that her early approval of the Third Reich was a source of keen embarrassment. As a result, she gave a rather odd story to the *Evening Standard* (2 February 1940), which began 'The Germans, before the war, were always very assiduous in their cultivation, for propaganda purposes, of important English women…' and continued to relate how she had been a habitual traveller to Germany for many years to take the 'cure' at Baden-Baden. Indeed, the article continued, she was now recovering from illness and her only dinner engagement this winter had been with Lord and Lady Halifax (he was the current Foreign Secretary and an unimpeachable character witness). This non-story seems a deliberate attempt to rehabilitate her pre-war German travels; there is no mention at all of Hitler or any politics.

To ensure no one could doubt her true allegiances she made a grand patriotic gesture, donating the cost of a Spitfire to the war effort. For a little under £6,000, the Spitfire P8643 *Margaret Helen* was built at Vickers Armstrong, Castle Bromwich, in March 1941. It saw active service from 21 May 1941 till 30 December 1944, when it was scrapped, having flown a number of sorties over France and sustained a great deal of accidental damage. Despite these vicissitudes, the plane always managed to bring her pilots back alive, even in the most dangerous circumstances.

Below: The Spitfire *Margaret Helen* was in service from May 1941 until December 1944.

The course of the war

Mrs Greville's male relatives joined up. William McEwan Younger, (1905–92), had joined the Royal Artillery in 1937, and in 1939 he became a major in the 40th Light Anti-aircraft Battery. In November 1940 he was sent to the Middle East, taking part in the siege of Tobruk, earning the DSO. He became a Lieutenant-Colonel, took part in the North African campaign, and landed in Salerno as part of the Italian campaign. He was known by his men as Colonel Screwtop, as the main supplier of beer to the army was the firm of McEwan Youngers. His cousin Henry Johnston Younger was less lucky; he was killed in action on 12 June 1940.

In May 1940 Winston Churchill succeeded Neville Chamberlain as Prime Minister. Winston's ability to state exactly what his audience felt was an inspirational gift. Physically frail and elderly as Mrs Ronnie now was, she had no compunction in telephoning Winston Churchill at Downing Street to offer her advice, having known him for nearly 40 years. She was often critical of the man who was to be the wartime saviour of Britain, but she also appreciated his sterling qualities: 'I think Winston is being quite wonderful...I think he is doing absolute marvels. His efforts are superhuman,' she wrote.

Although her eyesight was failing, and she had to dictate her letters, she kept abreast of political developments. Just before the fall of France in June 1940, she had heard that Monsieur Corbin, the former French Ambassador, was predicting that France might declare war on England. She wrote from Charles Street: 'I have never put any faith in France. I have enjoyed the French but I have always said France was the *cocotte* of Europe. I telephoned to Downing Street wondering if Winston knew what Corbin had said...'

The Queen commented 'I'm so glad we've been bombed. Now I can look the East End in the face'.

After the Dunkirk Evacuation Britain faced its gravest test, and the threat of invasion was believed to be imminent. The Luftwaffe stepped up its activities; on 13 September 1940 Buckingham Palace was bombed in broad daylight from a German plane that flew up the Mall. The Queen commented, 'I'm so glad we've been bombed. Now I can look the East End in the face.' She also learned to fire a revolver, intending to take a few of the enemy with her if need be.

The Dorchester in wartime

While the country awaited the German onslaught, Hector Bolitho, an old friend of Mrs Greville, remarked that the old ladies who used to reside in London had scuttled off to safer spots in Cornwall or Wales with their lapdogs. One old lady, however, scorned such an approach; just after Dunkirk, in July 1940, Mrs Greville moved permanently into the Dorchester Hotel. According to Beverley Nichols, her decision to move into the Dorchester was because she wished '…to establish herself, dying as she was, in the very centre of this city of terror, with its wailing, siren-haunted skies … because here she could exercise to the last and to the full her unique talent for malicious comment.'

She took an extensive suite occupying more than half of one of the topmost floors, with a view over Hyde Park, and established herself and her retinue with some style. Mrs Greville was preparing to go out with a bang.

The Dorchester Hotel on Park Lane was built of reinforced concrete, and had a deep basement and eight floors above ground. Completed in 1931, it was

Below: Advertisement for the Dorchester Hotel in *Harper's Bazaar* magazine, 1940. The hotel advertised itself as one of the safest buildings in London during the Second World War, with eight floors of heavily reinforced concrete each a foot thick and a gas-proof shelter underneath the hotel.

Harper's Bazaar for April 1940

One of the SAFEST buildings in LONDON

5

EIGHT FLOORS OF HEAVILY REINFORCED CONCRETE EACH ONE FOOT THICK

RESTAURANT AND OTHER PUBLIC ROOMS

THREE FOOT RAFT OF HEAVILY REINFORCED CONCRETE

GAS-PROOF SHELTER

THE newest hotel of the first order in London, The Dorchester incorporates all the plans and ideas which the most brilliant constructional engineers have conceived for exceptional strength and safety. As will be seen from this cross-section of the hotel structure, The Dorchester, with eight floors of almost indestructible concrete and in addition a 3-foot raft of concrete above the ground floor, is veritably bomb-proof.

It is quite impossible to obtain better hotel accommodation anywhere in the world, no matter what you pay

The DORCHESTER OVERLOOKING HYDE PARK
LONDON W.1

MAYfair 8888

ultra-modern and widely believed to be the safest hotel in London. It was certainly one of the quietest – the walls were lined with cork, and dried seaweed was used as sound-proofing between floors, which muffled the sound of explosions outside. In common with other substantial buildings in central London, the elegant, Art Deco entrance was screened by a wall of sandbags, the roof was covered with a layer of shingle as extra fire-proofing against incendiaries, and the luxurious curtains were interlined with blackout material. Fire-watchers were deployed on the roof to extinguish incendiary flares.

Mrs Greville was never happy to be seen in her wheelchair and she took advantage of a discreet side entrance to the hotel so that she did not have to traverse the crowded lobby. The hotel had become the fulcrum of London society; it was the place where power-brokers met, but it was also where the famous Lew Stone and his seven-piece dance band held sway from 1940 to 1942. Consequently, 'The Dorch' was at the heart of wartime London.

The Blitz

The concerted Blitz on London began in September 1940 and continued until 10 May 1941: strategic nocturnal bombing over nine months. After dark, when the entire city was blacked out, enemy aircraft filled the sky, heralded by the wail of air-raid sirens. On moonlit nights they navigated by the distinctive turns of the Thames. Bombing raids continued for hour after hour, the populace seeking shelter wherever they could. The streets were filled with the sounds of explosions, the air was thick with smoke and the searchlights attempted to pinpoint the bombers so that the guns on the ground could target them.

For Dorchester residents, the noise unleashed by the anti-aircraft guns in Hyde Park, just across the road, was appalling. Victor Cazalet, MP organised the informal use of the basement-level Turkish baths as a nocturnal air-raid shelter for the great and good who had taken up residence at the hotel. The residents dozed on beds placed behind screens to afford some semblance of privacy. What those in the Turkish baths did not know was that they were less than a foot (30 centimetres) under the tarmac covering the road surface of Park Lane. One bomb could have wiped them

all out. As the American war correspondent Ed Murrow remarked, '…at least you would be bombed with the right sort of people…'

Mrs Greville scorned the very idea of descending nightly to the air-raid shelters, preferring to sit out the barrage in the comfort of her large suite. She had a favourite chair next to the telephone, and during ferocious air raids, she had a teasing habit of placing internal phone calls to individual VIPs who had sought sanctuary in the basement. She would have her prey located by the hotel staff, and invite them to come and join her in her suite. 'But my *dear* Lord X, you really *must* come up. I am sure the air in that shelter is very bad, and I *know* you have a weak chest!' Few were brave enough to refuse her summons, but those who did were still branded as cowards by Maggie Greville.

> *Mrs Greville scorned the very idea of descending nightly to the air-raid shelters, preferring to sit out the barrage in the comfort of her large suite.*

Mrs Greville gave occasional dinner parties at the Dorchester. Food at the hotel was challenged by the rigours of rationing, as elsewhere, but Mrs Greville continued to entertain in some style, supplying the kitchens with eggs and cream from the Home Farm at Polesden Lacey.

Hanging on

In October 1941 and January 1942 Mrs Greville sent letters to her friends mentioning that she was recuperating at her country house; she had been so ill at the Dorchester on one occasion that her doctor had attended her throughout two nights in a row, and he had packed her off to Polesden Lacey until her strength returned.

She found her prolonged ill-health a nuisance; at last, she confirmed in a note to 'Birdie' Amery, she was allowed to sit in an armchair, but was bored and hoping to get back to London in the last week of January 1942. She must have rallied, as she couldn't avoid a sideswipe at Winston Churchill, who had been photographed at the controls of a plane: 'I do so wish the PM had not gone in for cheap publicity, smoking a cigar and pretending to preach in mid-Atlantic.'

Ill she may have been, but she nurtured and cherished her relationship with the royal household and would disperse nuggets of gossip to her circle. According to Leo Amery's diary the day after Chamberlain died in November 1940, Mrs Ronnie Greville had confided in him the 'great secret that Queen Elizabeth, voicing royal apprehension about [Churchill], had remarked that he was alright as a war Prime Minister, implying that she would not like him to be a peacetime one.' Mrs Greville also told Victor Cazalet that 'the King and Queen feel Winston puts them in the shade. He is always sending messages for the nation that the King ought to send...'

One typical dinner party in Mrs Greville's Dorchester suite at the height of the Blitz was fondly remembered by Beverley Nichols. Bole, the Head Steward, was a regular fixture, but on this occasion Bacon, the long-serving butler, and Hawkins, the first footman, had also come up from Polesden Lacey to attend the guests. Outside, bombs were falling and detonating, the anti-aircraft batteries were firing at the Luftwaffe and alarms and sirens were wailing. Inside, Mrs Greville was festooned in emeralds because one might as well wear them and go out in style.

She continued to entertain, and retained her fondness for royalty, inviting the dispossessed King of Greece to dine at the hotel in February 1942. (She had written: 'I do like him, even if he is an X-king'). Also present were 'Chips' Channon, and Dickie and Edwina Mountbatten, but the evening did not go with a swing; the ex-King said he could hardly look at food as it made him think of his starving compatriots. This put a damper on proceedings and, as a result, Chips noted, Mrs Greville seemed 'ageing and silent'.

The last formal lunch party she gave was on 30 April 1942, in her suite at the Dorchester Hotel. She was now in a wheelchair all the time, and in pain, but took the opportunity to wear an astonishing array of her finest jewels. Guests included Lord Louis Mountbatten who had been appointed Chief of Combined Operations, his wife Edwina, the Duke and Duchess of Kent, the Duchess of Buccleuch, Brendan Bracken and 'Chips' Channon – she greeted him with the words, 'Chips is my only vice.' She was still very *au courant* with affairs at the Palace, and relished gossip; the Queen had visited her recently at the hotel.

For the last time, in the summer of 1942 Mrs Greville made the long and difficult journey to Scotland, and joined the King and Queen at Balmoral for tea on 16 August. Sir Alan Lascelles, the King's adviser, recorded in his diary that he had to help manoeuvre her wheelchair into the dining room, an operation that came to an abrupt halt when the Queen's dog was sick in the chair's path. Sir Alan was not fond of Mrs Greville; '…she has been a constant mischief-maker for twenty-five years, but I don't think she will make much more now.'

Outside, bombs were falling and detonating, anti-aircraft batteries were firing at the Luftwaffe and alarms and sirens were wailing. Inside, Mrs Greville was festooned in emeralds because one might as well wear them and go out in style.

The Royal Family, Mrs Greville and their mutual friends received a profound shock only days later. On 25 August 1942 the Duke of Kent was killed in a plane crash while on active service in Scotland; he had been flying to Iceland to inspect RAF installations when the pilot became disorientated in mist and flew into a mountain. The sudden loss was hard to bear; the Duke, handsome and urbane, had had a spectacularly raffish youth, but he had become extremely popular since his marriage to the beautiful Princess Marina of Greece in 1934, attended by Mrs Greville. The King and Queen were deeply distraught; they had been staying at Balmoral, but returned to Windsor for the funeral, which was held on 29 August. The King found the funeral service for his beloved brother almost unbearable, as did Noël Coward, who had been the Duke's close friend for nineteen years. The grief and strain on all concerned was appalling; Queen Mary had lost one son, John, as an adolescent, and more recently had been estranged from her eldest, David, following the Abdication. To have her beloved George killed in this way was almost unimaginable. Queen Elizabeth returned to Balmoral and succumbed to bronchitis, spending weeks in bed convalescing. Significantly 'Chips' Channon, another great friend of the Duke of Kent, subsequently claimed to have lost his diary during the weeks after the death, and did not resume making his entries until 19 September. As a result, there is no record from Chips of the death of either the Duke or, just three weeks later, of Margaret Greville.

Death and Legacy

"...[Mrs Ronnie] insisted that she was in pain (though the doctors denied this) and told me that she wished to die..."

(Osbert Sitwell, writing to Queen Elizabeth on 16 September 1942.)

The last days of Margaret Greville

When Beverley Nichols visited his old friend at the Dorchester in September 1942, he found her bedridden, frail and shrunken. She was wearing her famous diamond rings, but she had become so thin that she had to clench her hands to keep them on her fingers. She was glad to see him, as there was an air raid in progress and some of her acquaintances were not even willing to risk leaving the air-raid shelter under the hotel to see her.

It was evident that her physical strength was fading; she had little appetite even for malicious gossip. When leaving he wished her '*au revoir*'. But she shook her head and replied, 'I think not, my dear…I think it is goodbye.' With that, a bomb fell nearby and Margaret Greville whispered, 'That damned Ribbentrop. Thank God I told him what I thought of him when he came to Polesden. I told him that if ever there was a war, he might beat the English, but he would never beat the Scots.' She fell into an uneasy sleep and Nichols left her for the last time.

Left: Mrs Ronnie's desk at Polesden Lacey; here, surrounded by photographs of her family and friends, she organised her intricate business and social life.

Osbert Sitwell was faithful to his old friend till the end. The day after her death at the Dorchester Hotel he wrote a simple but heartfelt letter to the Queen, which began, 'I thought perhaps your Majesty would want to hear the details of Mrs Ronnie's death; she was so devoted to the King and Your Majesty.'

He described how Mrs Greville had refused to eat for a week, before rallying slightly at the weekend. On the Sunday she had a cerebral thrombosis, which left her in a coma. Throughout the Monday, Osbert stayed with, but she did not regain consciousness. She had no close relatives present, only Bole, her Head Steward and Aline, her elderly French maid, both of whom were overwrought, so Osbert attended the doctor's conference on Monday evening. They discussed and then rejected a surgical procedure to tackle the thrombosis, on the grounds that she would have been unlikely to survive the operation.

She died at 2am on Tuesday 15 September 1942. The faithful Francis Bole was present at her deathbed, and the death certificate was issued by her personal physician, Alexander McCall of Wimpole Street. According to her death certificate, she had slipped into a coma, having suffered a cerebral thrombosis. Contributory factors were arterio-sclerosis, nephritis and 'dilatation of heart'. Her age on the death certificate is given as 75, though she was in fact three months away from her 79th birthday.

Sir Alan Lascelles, who saw the news on his arrival in London on the night-train from Scotland, remarked in his diary: 'Mrs Ronnie Greville is dead of an apoplexy.' He followed this bald statement with a phrase in Greek, taken from Homer's *Odyssey*, meaning 'So may perish anyone else who does such a deed'.

Her age on the death certificate is given as 75, though she was in fact three months away from her 79th birthday.

Tributes

Not all her social circle were so judgemental. Sir John Simon, who had once asked her to marry him, wrote a poignant appreciation, which appeared in *The Times* on 17 September: 'There must be many, very many among Mrs Greville's innumerable friends and close acquaintants who, learning of her death on Monday, have a poignant feeling of distress that there is no one – neither husband, nor child, nor brother, nor sister – to whom to send a message of sympathy and condolence.'

He wrote approvingly of Mrs Greville's 'Scottish downrightness in her judgments which, whether you approved them or not, was the mark of an utterly honest creature ... Now that release has come to her from her long and torturing illness, borne with such fortitude and patience, we would not willingly let this gracious and generous spirit pass from the earth without some word of affectionate farewell.' His affection for her was genuine; Osbert Sitwell was surprised to discover five years after her death that Sir John often visited her grave.

Osbert's tribute to Mrs Greville in the same paper was heartfelt; he admired her wit and intelligence, her lack of pretension, and her ability to judge character shrewdly. Interestingly, both men took the opportunity to commend her patriotism, and her particular pride in being Scottish; it being wartime, they may have been hoping to mitigate any criticism of her earlier misplaced enthusiasms for what were now Britain's enemies. Sir John Simon went so far as to say, 'her courage never failed her and was conspicuous during the worst of the bombing attacks on London' (*The Times*, 17 September 1942).

Mrs Greville's funeral

The King and Queen were represented at Mrs Greville's funeral by Sir Eric Miéville. The service was held at Great Bookham Church on 19 September 1942, but Mrs Greville had instructed that her body was to be interred in the Lady's Garden at Polesden Lacey. The mourners included Lord and Lady Simon, the Belgian Ambassador, Lord Greville, The Hon. Mrs Roland Cubitt, Lord Beaverbrook, Mr Hore-Belisha, 'Chips' Channon, some of her Younger relatives, the faithful Bole, Adeline Liron, and many of her staff. Sir Osbert Sitwell found the occasion harrowing, and he wrote to the Queen:

Below: **Sir Osbert Sitwell.**

I never saw Polesden look so pretty as it did on the day of the funeral; quite lovely. Mrs Ronnie was buried in that green space between the kitchen garden and house, enclosed by yew hedges...it was dreadfully sad though; so sad because she had no near relations.

'Chips' Channon also attended the memorial service on 24 September at St Mark's, North Audley Street in London. This was the same church in which Maggie had married Ronnie, 51 years before. On this occasion, it was 'crowded with Ambassadors and all the usual funeral faces', 106 titled and official names, many of them representing the Royal Family, as well as her staff. 'Chips' took Sacheverell and Georgia Sitwell and the Carisbrookes to lunch at Claridge's afterwards, where they reminisced about Mrs Greville's acerbic wit over three bottles of Moselle, and speculated who would inherit the famous Greville jewels.

The Queen was among the first to know Mrs Greville's intentions, and it seems to have come as a regrettable surprise to her, though she put a brave face on it. A few days after the funeral, the Queen was told that the National Trust was to acquire the estate of Polesden Lacey, the art, the contents of both houses, and a substantial endowment. Writing from Balmoral on 30 September 1942 to the King, she said that Mrs Greville's solicitor, Gerald Russell, had:

...brought with him an extract from her will just saying that she left me her jewels with her 'loving thoughts', and twenty thousand pounds to Margaret Rose. These are free of death duties. Polesden she left to the National Trust with money to keep it up, this is secret at the moment so don't tell anybody. I am not sure that this isn't a very good idea because it is a very difficult place to keep up, terribly expensive I believe and needing a millionaire owner...this, Darling, is all I know and I write it to you because I don't like to broadcast it on the telephone. Perhaps it is just as well, things being as they are, that she has done this...

There is a palpable sense of disappointment about the fate of Polesden Lacey. On 16 November 1942 Queen Mary wrote Queen Elizabeth an affectionate letter:

How kind of Mrs Greville to leave you her jewels, and she had some lovely pearls and nice emeralds too I think...I hope that the jewels will make up for the loss of Polesden Lacey, I am sorry she altered her will but perhaps it would have been a white elephant to Bertie. I can understand your pleasure about the jewels, you are right not to say anything about them...

Above: The Picture Corridor at Polesden Lacey was used by Mrs Greville to show a selection from her impressive art collection. On her death, the National Trust added the best of the paintings from her London home to the display.

The will

*"Everybody else leaves their money to the poor.
I am going to leave it to the rich."*

London buzzed with gossip about Mrs Greville's estate
following her death. She had used her enormous wealth
all her life to divide and rule, and in arranging her affairs
she continued the habit. She had dropped hints to the
favoured few during her lifetime; she had used Polesden
Lacey as a bargaining chip to become close to the Royal
Family, and then changed her mind, and she had
announced her intention to leave her pearls to the Queen.
After tax, her net fortune came to £1,505,120 5s 10d,
an amount worth approximately £39,000,000 in today's
values. Death duties amounted to £830,120.

*She had used her
enormous wealth all her
life to divide and rule, and
in arranging her affairs
she continued the habit.*

Her will, dated 27 March 1942, makes fascinating reading. She appointed
four executors, and left them each £5,000. To her personal maid, 'my
valued friend, Marie Adeline Liron', she left all her clothes, two rows of
cultured pearls, and any pieces of jewellery under £100 each in value.
Adeline Liron was to receive a tax-free sum of £50 a month for the rest
of her life. She was left Mrs Greville's dogs and allocated a sum of £100
per annum after tax to provide for the pets. Mrs Greville also provided her
with a home at Polesden, in her employer's former apartments, for life.

Individual legacies included a generous sum of £1,000 and an annuity
of £500 for life to Francis Bole. He also was given the modern household
silver. Sidney Smith, the chauffeur, received an annuity of £200 for life,
and was left all her motorcars, their accessories and the garage furniture at
11, Hay's Mews, at the back of the Charles Street property. George Moss,
the head butler, had £100 a year for life. Gladys Yealland, the personal
maid, had a legacy of £500.

To every one of her servants, who had been in her service for more than
six months and less than eight years, she left two years' wages. There were
28 people who qualified and were still employed by her at the time of her
death. For the eight members of staff who had been in her service for more

than eight years, she left each a generous seven years' salary. Two of her staff had joined the armed forces but they were also remembered in her will, and the widow of one of her former employees, Mrs Hart, who occupied a cottage on Goldstone Farm at Polesden, was granted the use of it free of rent for her lifetime.

Bequests to her social circle were extremely generous. 'Her Royal Highness Princess Margaret Rose, of Buckingham Palace' was left £20,000. Mrs Greville had favoured the second child, knowing that her elder sister Princess Elizabeth would be better off. Queen Ena of Spain, now exiled, widowed and living abroad in very reduced circumstances, was to get £25,000, '…with deep affection and in memory of the great kindness and affection which Her Majesty has shown me.' Ten godchildren, including Rosalind Cubitt, daughter of Sonia Keppel, were each left £500. Sonia received £2,000.

Her relatives William McEwan Younger and Major Ralph Younger each had a legacy of 30,000 ordinary shares in Scottish Brewers Ltd. Lady Reay, who had been Charlotte Younger until her marriage, got £1,000 and her daughter, the Honourable Margaret Anne Mackay, born only in March 1941, Mrs Greville's youngest goddaughter, was left £5,000. 'Small reminders of our friendship' of £1,000 each went to the Countess of Ilchester, Lady Simon and the Duchess of Buccleuch.

Mrs Greville's two favourite doctors, both of whom were Scots, were left £5,000 each. To various institutions and charities there were many bequests, reflecting her lifelong interests. The National Anti-Vivisection League was awarded £10,000, 'which I hope the Society will in some way appropriate use for the protection of dogs'. Guy's Hospital was left £1,000, as was the nearby Newcomen Day Nursery in Southwark and the Provincial Police Orphanage. The Royal Sailors Rest, the RSPCA and National Canine Defence League were left £500 each. The Battersea Dogs Home, the Home of Rest for Horses and the London and Western Servants Orphanage each received £100. She left £1,000 to the Edinburgh Working Men's Club and Institute in Edinburgh.

Mrs Greville's two favourite doctors, both of whom were Scots, were left £5,000 each.

Osbert Sitwell, her longstanding friend, received a bequest that transformed his existence and left him, according to Nancy Mitford, 'on top of the world'. He wrote to Queen Elizabeth: 'Dear Mrs Ronnie left me a legacy of ten thousand pounds and I feel enormously rich. I've always been a "remittance man" or a wage-earner before and have never had a penny in the bank…' His brother, Sacheverell, who had been a frequent guest of Mrs Greville's, received nothing, though his son Reresby was left £1,000. One loyal friend who surprisingly was excluded from the will was Beverley Nichols; Mrs Greville had carried out her threat of leaving him out of her will because he had not agreed to stand as an MP against Duff Cooper in 1931, as she had wanted.

The Greville Bequest

It was the disposition of certain of her jewellery that caused the greatest amazement. 'Her Majesty Queen Elizabeth, Buckingham Palace – with all my loving thoughts all my jewels and jewellery…' This bequest included all her jewellery valued at more than £100 apiece, and therefore comprised

Below: **Children at the Newcomen Street Day Nursery, 1926, which was remembered in Mrs Greville's will.**

some 60 items, including the emeralds, which once belonged to the Empress Josephine, the exquisite Boucheron diamond tiara, a diamond ring and several sets of pendant earrings, diamond clips and other ornaments. These were conveyed to Queen Elizabeth in a small black lacquered tin trunk, emblazoned in gold with the initials 'M.H.G.' and the address, Polesden Lacey, Dorking.

These were Mrs Greville's favourite pieces; the earliest was the Greville Bow Brooch, in silver and gold with diamonds, an enormous piece measuring some 12 x 10 cm, which she had commissioned from Boucheron in May 1900. Most spectacular was the Greville Tiara, made by Boucheron of Paris in 1921, of diamonds on a lightweight platinum frame, remodelled from a diadem made for Mrs Greville by the same firm in 1901. This was entirely geometric in form, with an abstract honeycomb motif. Always aware of her diminutive size, Queen Elizabeth had Cartier add some clusters of diamonds to the front section in 1953, to increase the height of the piece; it remained one of her favourite tiaras, and has been frequently worn in more recent years by Camilla, Duchess of Cornwall. Both Queen Elizabeth and

Below: **The small tin trunk containing Mrs Greville's bequest of magnificent jewellery which she left to Queen Elizabeth in 1942.**

the Duchess of Cornwall were to wear the Greville Festoon Necklace, often with the Greville Tiara, a spectacular five-row diamond necklace created by Cartier of London as two co-ordinating separate pieces, one of three rows and the other of two, in 1929 and 1938.

Some of Mrs Greville's jewels were charming in their freshness; a matching pair of ivy-leaf clips in diamonds and platinum by Cartier were passed on to Princess Elizabeth by her parents to mark her 21st birthday in 1947. In the same year, the Princess was given the Greville Chandelier Earrings, to celebrate her wedding. These were a phenomenal set of 32 diamonds mounted in platinum, each of which had been selected by Cartier in 1929 for the brilliance and unique charm of its cut. The design was geometric in the hard-edged and brilliant Art Deco style of its day; Princess Elizabeth wore these earrings for formal occasions in the 1950s and 1960s, but their size and flamboyance may not have suited her taste thereafter; instead, both the Queen Mother and later her daughter preferred the Greville Peardrop Earrings, a superficially simple pair of enormous pendant diamond earrings, each weighing over 20 carats, commissioned by Mrs Greville through the New York branch of Cartier and delivered by the London branch of the firm on 31 May 1938.

Above: **The Greville peardrop earrings.**

It is intriguing that Mrs Greville left such an enormous bequest to just one person; but in fact Queen Elizabeth owned only a limited range of jewellery. When she was being photographed by Cecil Beaton in 1939, he asked her to put on as much jewellery as she had

...a matching pair of ivy-leaf clips in diamonds and platinum by Cartier were passed on Princess Elizabeth by her parents to mark her 21st birthday in 1947.

available. 'The choice isn't very great, you know,' she replied with an apologetic smile. Mostly she wore gifts from her family and her husband, given on her marriage or anniversaries. In 1936 Mrs Greville had given her a magnificent three-strand set of pearls, which she wore extensively throughout the war and afterwards, but many of the pieces that had previously belonged to Queen Alexandra were still in the care of Queen Mary, who was determined to hang on to them for her own use, as well as the colossal jewels she had been given on her State visit to India. Queen Mary had therefore designated very few pieces 'belonging to the Crown and to be worn by all future queens', to use Queen Victoria's phrase. By leaving a treasure chest to the young Queen, Mrs Greville was aware that she would make the old Queen happy too, as Mary would not have to relinquish the jewels she adored until she no longer needed them.

Magnificent though these jewels were, it was some time before they were seen again in public. In wartime, it was felt that wearing spectacular jewellery would be in bad taste while the general public at home and the armed forces overseas were suffering such hardship. When the war ended, the mood of austerity prevailed, so the first outing for the Boucheron tiara, now renamed the Greville Tiara, was not until 1947 when the Queen wore it in South Africa.

Camilla, Duchess of Cornwall has worn the Greville Tiara, and her engagement ring was remodelled from one of the Greville bequest. The Duchess is a direct descendant of Alice Keppel, and through her marriage to Prince Charles, great-great-grandson of Edward VII, now she wears the jewels once owned by her great-grandmother's friend.

Camilla, Duchess of Cornwall has worn the Greville Tiara, and her engagement ring was remodelled from one of the Greville bequest.

'Left to the nation'

Mrs Greville had spoken of leaving her possessions and a substantial bequest 'to the nation'. When it was formally announced on 25 November 1942 that the National Trust had been left her estate at Polesden Lacey as well as many of the contents of Charles Street and a substantial endowment, 'for use by the public, as a memorial to her father, Mr William McEwan', as *The Guardian* put it, there was considerable comment.

At its inception, the National Trust had had no intention of taking on country houses; it was created to care for 'Places of Historic Interest or Natural Beauty'. But by the 1930s it was apparent that many country houses had been destroyed, sold or broken up, due to a decline in agricultural rents, the imposition of death duties and increased taxation. A number of landed families had lost their heirs – indeed, successive heirs – in the carnage of the Great War. There were also those who, born to privilege, felt they should make what they owned available to everyone.

Therefore in 1937 the National Trust's legal status was expanded so it could look after houses, and ensure the 'preservation of furniture, pictures and chattels of any description having national or historic or artistic interest'.

Nevertheless, it was a bold move. Mrs Greville left to the charity the estate of Polesden Lacey, with its collections, and those of her London house, with a very large bequest. She specified in her will: 'That all my pictures and objects [sic] d'art in my house, no. 16 Charles Street, or elsewhere...shall be taken to Polesden Lacey and added to those already there...so as to form a Picture and Art Gallery in a suitable part or parts of the house...'

Above: Camilla, Duchess of Cornwall, granddaughter of Mrs Ronnie's goddaughter Sonia, wearing the Greville Tiara and the Greville Necklace at the Queen's Commonwealth Dinner in Kampala in 2007.

Cataloguing the bequest

James Lees-Milne, who had joined the National Trust as secretary to the newly formed Country House Committee in 1936, first heard of the bequest on 18 September 1942, and spent much of the following autumn and winter dealing with the massive acquisition. He attended a meeting with her executors, and he was staggered at the size and value of the estate, initially estimated as being worth £2 million. 'Everyone in London is agog to learn the terms of Mrs G.'s will. She was a lady who loved the great because they were great, and apparently had a tongue dipped in gall. I remember old Lady Leslie once exclaiming, when her name was mentioned, "Maggie Greville! I would sooner have an open sewer in my drawing-room!"...'

James Lees-Milne was faced with organising the acceptance of the bequest, and sought specialist help in identifying which items from both houses were to be displayed at Polesden for display, and which would be sold. Merging the contents of two large houses and selling what was superfluous was a considerable challenge in wartime Britain. In October 1942 he explored Polesden, and his visit to Charles Street three weeks later was a revelation – 'It is a palace,' he wrote. As the house had been closed up for the duration of hostilities, Lees-Milne was faced with sorting through all the furniture which had been stacked in the drawing room and covered in dustsheets. Francis Bole showed the National Trust party over the house; he was apparently 'very drunk and lachrymose', and could be heard sobbing quietly in the background. He had worked for Mrs Greville for 42 years; they were friends as well as mistress and employee, and he was the man she had entrusted with the task of destroying her private papers after her death.

Not everyone remembered Mrs Greville with so much affection; Harold Nicolson in conversation with Lees-Milne in November

Below: **Large porcelain 'famille rose' vase and cover with Dog of Fo (c.1760), just one of the many treasures bequeathed by Mrs Ronnie to the National Trust at Polesden Lacey.**

1942 recalled her as a 'common, waspish woman who got where she did through persistence and money', who had 'built herself a fictitious reputation for cleverness, and was not even witty...'. Harold Nicolson dropped in at Charles Street when Lees-Milne was there cataloguing the collection in January 1943, was charming to the formidable housekeeper Mrs Reid, and 'strode up and down the stone hall nostalgically but unregretfully recalling the awful parties he had attended in this house...'. Similarly, Lady Crewe 'related gleefully if inaccurately' that Mrs Greville's mother had been the wife of the day-porter at McEwan's brewery, and that Mr McEwan had put him on night duty 'for convenience'.

Christie's the auctioneers produced a comprehensive inventory for each property, the paintings were initially assessed by Sir Alec Martin, Managing Director of the same firm, and James Lees-Milne spent New Year's Day going through the Charles Street inventory, deciding what to keep and what to sell. Both Mr Abbey of Christie's and Trenchard Cox, expert custodian from the Wallace Collection, were disappointed by the quality of some of the French furniture, but the early silver was very impressive and so were many of the Chinese ceramics.

Kenneth Clark, who had known Mrs Greville well, advised on the paintings. H. Clifford Smith, former Keeper of Furniture and Woodwork at the Victoria and Albert Museum, was given the task of identifying objects deemed to be of such 'national, scientific, historic or artistic interest' to exempt them from death duties so long as they were to go to one of the national museums or the National Trust.

His investigation of Charles Street took three days, and was complicated by the fact that the contents of the ballroom and drawing room, and all the paintings in the house, had been stacked in the dining room for safety's sake. He added to the list of objects that should be kept, and was impressed by the 40 pieces of old English silver, the 16 panels of tapestry, and an Adam-Chippendale commode similar to two examples by Robert Adam at Osterley Park. He also found five small sixteenth- and seventeenth-century Italian bronzes on ebony or marble stands in the safe, and added them to the list. There were a large number of fine blue and white Chinese ceramics, a collection of 28 miniature paintings, and Mrs Greville's orders and decorations.

Harold Nicolson... 'strode up and down the stone hall nostalgically but unregretfully recalling the awful parties he had attended in this house...'

Surplus goods

The sale of the magnificent cellars from both houses caused excitement in war-torn Britain, cut off from European vintners and wine merchants. On 22 March 1943, Christie's auction rooms were packed with 200 dealers for the sale of Mrs Greville's fine wines, liqueurs and champagne. Up for auction were 1,000 bottles of claret, and 6 rare bottles of Grande Champagne 1810 brandy. Mr Bole, the Head Steward, who had nurtured and cared for the cellars for more than four decades, collected and kept press cuttings relating to this sale.

Many people dropped hints about getting access to Mrs Greville's houses now she was dead. Some people were practical; Miss Paterson, of the Trust, hoped that the charity would be able to retain Charles Street's considerable

Below: **The study at Polesden Lacey was designed by Mewès and Davis as a private room for Mrs Greville. The mahogany writing desk in the bow window is English c.1800, but other surplus furniture was sold at auction in 1943.**

stock of pre-war cleaning materials, such as soap, mops and brooms, now impossible to buy, for use in other properties. Lees-Milne himself pocketed 'like a thief in the night, a broom, a brush and a cake of scrubbing soap'. Gerry Villiers dropped in at Charles Street hoping to buy a stair-carpet but was unsuccessful, and left with some lightbulbs. 'Chips' Channon begged Lees-Milne to locate and return to him a bloodstone he had given to Mrs Greville, but he refused.

Tancred Borenius, affable art expert, offered to 'help' in assessing the paintings, talked volubly of Mrs Greville's shortcomings, and was politely turned away. Heavy hints were also dropped through an intermediary, Puss Gaskell, that Queen Mary would like nothing more than to visit Polesden and 'play around'. 'Thank God, she can't,' wrote the beleaguered Lees-Milne in his diary.

Lees-Milne himself pocketed 'like a thief in the night, a broom, a brush and a cake of scrubbing soap'.

'I am heartily sick of that deceased lady,' wrote James Lees-Milne in May 1943. Nevertheless, he arranged with Kenneth Clark for a number of her paintings to be loaned to the National Gallery for an exhibition in the summer of 1943. Gradually the house inched towards completion; the surplus furniture from Polesden Lacey was taken away at the very end of August 1943 and sold at auction. The two-day sale at Christie's realised more than £8,000. A Chippendale-style mahogany settee covered with needlework brought 135 guineas; four large Oriental carpets were fiercely fought over; and a Louis XVI parquetry commode made 350 guineas.

It is believed that some of Mrs Greville's superfluous furniture was bought at auction by the Foreign Office and shipped to Government House in Nassau, the official residence of the Duke and Duchess of Windsor. To keep the Duke out of trouble and away from any contact with Nazi Germany, Winston Churchill had appointed him Governor of the Bahamas in 1940, a post both the Windsors loathed, but tolerated until 1945. They had complained vociferously about the quality of their official accommodation on the island, so it is ironic to think that major improvements to their comfort could be traced to the *largesse* of Mrs Greville, whom they had so disliked.

'…utterly Mrs Ronald Greville…'

In an imaginative move, it was suggested by Sir Edgar Bonham-Carter of the National Trust that Polesden Lacey should be shown as an Edwardian lady's country house, rather than as a museum. Personal touches reflecting her activities and character, her social circle and day-to-day activities would add to the place rather than detract from it. The house finally opened to the public in 1948; Robin Fedden wrote eloquently about it in *Country Life* in March 1948, commenting on how redolent the place was of the personality of Mrs Greville, because she had left everything, not just her magnificent works of art, but also the 'thousand and one unconsidered objects, from waste-paper baskets to pen-wipers, that precisely retain an atmosphere and which, at a later date, can rarely be assembled with any success even by the labours of the antiquarian and collector.'

Indeed, her personality is still very apparent at Polesden Lacey. Beverley Nichols visited on a day it was open to the public, toured the house, and reminisced about his old friend, a bittersweet experience. He eavesdropped on a conversation he had heard between two ladies, discussing Mrs Greville:

'Did you ever see her?'

'Yes, once, driving in her motor. She wasn't anything much to look at. Common, I thought – on the stout side, with grey hair. She had the Queen of Spain with her. Now, there was a lady.'

'It's funny, isn't it, giving this house to the nation, with everything in it, just as it was, for ever?'

The other nodded. 'Vanity I call it. Why, I'm told they even put the same flowers she used to like, in the vases and they've kept her big quill pen just where she left it, on her desk.'

'Well, really! Her pen! As if she were Napoleon!'

'But she was a sort of Napoleon,' I felt like telling them. 'A social Napoleon. They don't make women like that nowadays. She wasn't beautiful, she was brilliant, she was a fabulous snob. And yet, one had been genuinely fond of her.'

(All I could Never Be, *Beverley Nichols*)

Margaret Greville was indeed a 'social Napoleon'; she rose from obscure origins to conquer through personal charm and considerable cunning. Over seven decades, she used her wit and intelligence to advance her interests, to pursue power and influence and to position herself at the centre of any group of influence. She cultivated monarchs, collected the brilliant and met the dynamic figures of the age. She was drawn to power, she was adept at puncturing pomposity and bombast, but also used her considerable wealth quietly to fund education for those who couldn't afford it, and provide medical care for the needy. Capable of great kindness, she was a good friend though an implacable enemy.

Above: **Mrs Greville seated under the south portico at Polesden Lacey.**

Above all, she did her utmost to live according to her own truths, reinventing herself as necessary. She concealed the unpalatable facts of her own parentage until both her mother and father were dead, but she wanted the truth acknowledged after her time. Accustomed to covering her tracks, she arranged for her private papers to be destroyed, yet she wished to leave a memorial to her fascinating life in the most public way, accessible to anyone.

Though constantly surrounded by a cast of servants and friends, she was fundamentally alone for much of her adult life. It is hardly surprising that she was a mass of contradictions. As Queen Elizabeth wrote, in a letter to Sir Osbert Sitwell on 27 September 1942, 'I shall miss her very much indeed … she was so shrewd, so kind and so amusingly <u>un</u>kind, so sharp, such fun, so naughty … altogether a real person, a character, utterly Mrs Ronald Greville…'

'I shall miss her very much indeed … she was so shrewd, so kind and so amusingly <u>un</u>kind, so sharp, such fun, so naughty … altogether a real person, a character, utterly Mrs Ronald Greville…'

Acknowledgements

Researching 'Mrs Ronnie's' life was fascinating, but not straightforward. A great many people were extremely helpful and generous in sharing their knowledge and expertise. I would especially like to thank the following individuals, who contributed to this book in so many ways:

Grant Berry; Laura Brudenell; Pam Burbridge; Marie Chevant; Pamela Clark, Senior Archivist, and her colleagues at the Royal Archives; Roger Coleman; Paul Dearn; Harvey Edgington; Glyn Evans; Sarah Evans; Mrs Cynthia M. Flittner; Cathy Gosling; Ian Killeen; David Kitt; Alastair Laing; Duncan Little; Sue Lovett; Jonathan Marsh; Terry Megennis and Roy Tanner of GVA Grimley Ltd.; Vicky Nutt; Claudine Sablier Paquet, of Boucheron, Paris; Alan Parris; Clare Paterson and her colleagues at the University of Glasgow Archives; Steve Price, Kristy Richardson; Christopher Rowell; Chris Rowlin; Francesca Scoones; Andrea Selley; John Stachiewicz; Lauren Taylor; Alma Topen, and Bill Whitman.

Most importantly, I must thank the staff, volunteers and interns at Polesden Lacey, past and present, who made every possible effort to help tell this tale, because they felt the remarkable story of 'Mrs Ronnie' should be better known. Their enthusiasm was infectious, and their contributions were greatly appreciated.

Permissions

The author and publisher are grateful for the permission of Her Majesty Queen Elizabeth II to use material from the Royal Archives at Windsor Castle. The following archives and sources were also particularly helpful in granting permissions; Reading Papers, the British Library; Archives Boucheron de Paris; Churchill Papers, the Churchill Archives Centre, Cambridge; Windsor Castle; Cherwell Papers, Nuffield College, Oxford; The English-Speaking Union; Special Collections, Main Library, University of Birmingham; Scottish Brewing Archive, the University of Glasgow.

Picture Credits

Bibliography and Further Reading

Amory, Mark: **Lord Berners: The Last Eccentric** (Chatto & Windus, 1998)

Barron, Andrew: **Gossip: 1920 – 1970** (Hamish Hamilton, London, 1978)

Beaton, Cecil: **Self Portrait with Friends; the Selected Diaries of Cecil Beaton, 1926–1974**, edited by Richard Buckle (Weidenfeld and Nicholson, 1979)

Birkenhead, The Earl of: **The Prof in Two Worlds: The Official Life of Professor F.A. Lindemann, Viscount Cherwell** (Collins, 1961)

Birmingham, Stephen: **Duchess: The Story of Wallis Simpson** (Macmillan London Ltd., 1982)

Bloch, Michael: **Ribbentrop** (Bantam Press, 1994; this edition published by Abacus, 2003)

Bloch, Michael: **James Lees-Milne: The Life** (John Murray, 2009)

Bolitho, Hector: **War in the Strand** (Eyre and Spottiswoode, London, 1942)

Boothby, Lord: **Boothby: Recollections of a Rebel** (Hutchinson, 1978)

Bradford, Sarah: **George VI** (Weidenfeld and Nicolson, London, 1989)

Brendon, Piers: **The Dark Valley: A Panorama of the 1930s** (Jonathan Cape, London, 2000)

Bruce Lockhart, Sir Robert: **Your England** (Putnam, London, 1955)

Charmley, John: **Duff Cooper: the Authorized Biography** (Weidenfeld and Nicolson, London, 1986)

Chisholm, Anne: **Nancy Cunard** (Sidgwick and Jackson, London, 1977)

Clark, Kenneth: **Another Part of the Wood** (John Murray (Publishers) Ltd., 1974; this edition published by Coronet, 1976)

De Courcy, Anne: **Debs at War** (Weidenfeld and Nicolson, 2005; this edition published by Phoenix, 2006)

Freud, Clement: **Freud Ego** (BBC Worldwide Ltd., 2001).

Fromm, Bella: **Blood & Banquets: A Berlin Social Diary** (Carol Publishing Group, 1990)

Gardiner, Juliet: **The Edwardian Country House** (Channel 4 Books, an imprint of Pan Macmillan Ltd., 2002)

Greig, Geordie: **The King Maker: The Man who Saved George VI** (Hodder & Stoughton Ltd. 2011)

Griffiths, Richard: **Fellow Travellers of the Right: British Enthusiasts for Nazi Germany 1933–39** (Constable and Company Ltd)

Hart-Davis, Duff: **King's Counsellor: Abdication and War: The Diaries of Sir Alan Lascelles** (Weidenfeld and Nicolson, 2006)

Hattersley, Roy: **The Edwardians** (Little, Brown, 2004; this edition published by Abacus, 2006)

Higham, Charles: **Mrs Simpson: Secret Lives of the Duchess of Windsor** (First published as 'Wallis: Secret Lives of the Duchess of Windsor' by Sidgwick and Jackson Ltd., 1988; this edition published by Pan Books, 2005)

James, Robert Rhodes: **'Chips': The Diaries of Sir Henry Channon** (Weidenfeld & Nicolson, 1967; new paperback edition, 1993)

Jennings, Charles: **Them and Us: The American Invasion of British High Society** (Sutton Publishing, 2007)

Keppel, Sonia: **Edwardian Daughter** (Hamish Hamilton, London, 1958)

Lees-Milne, James: **Ancestral Voices: Diaries 1942–1943** (Michael Russell, 2003)

Lees-Milne, James: **Harold Nicolson: A Biography: Vol II 1930–1968** (Chatto & Windus, 1981)

Londonderry, the Marchioness of: **Retrospect** (Frederick Muller Ltd., 1938)

Masters, Brian: **Great Hostesses** (Constable and Company Ltd., 1982)

McLeod, Kirsty: **Battle Royal: Edward VIII and George VI – Brother Against Brother** (Constable and Company Ltd., 1999)

Meylan, Vincent: **Archives Secrètes Boucheron** (Editions SW Télémaque)

Mordaunt Crook, J.: **The Rise of the Nouveaux Riches** (John Murray, 1999)

Mosley, Sir Oswald: **My Life** (Thomas Nelson and Sons Ltd., 1968)

Nichols, Beverley: **The Sweet and Twenties** (Weidenfeld and Nicolson, 1958)

Nichols, Beverley: **All I Could Never Be** (Jonathan Cape, 1949)

Nichols, Beverley: **Twenty-Five** (Jonathan Cape, 1926; this edition published by Penguin Books, 1935)

Nichols, Beverley: **The Unforgiving Minute** (W.H. Allen, London, 1978)

Nicolson, Harold: **Diaries and Letters: 1930–1939** (First published 1966; this edition published by Fontana Books, 1969)

Nicholson, Juliet: **The Perfect Summer: Dancing into Shadow in 1911** (John Murray, 2006)

Pearson, John: Façades: **Edith, Osbert and Sacheverell Sitwell** (Fontana Paperbacks 1980; first published by Macmillan, London Ltd., 1978)

Plumptre, George: **The Fast Set: The World of Edwardian Racing** (André Deutsch Ltd., 1985)

Priestley, J. B: **The Edwardians** (Heinemann, 1970)

Pugh, Martin: **'Hurrah for the Blackshirts!' Fascists and Fascism in Britain between the Wars** (Jonathan Cape, 2005)

Rhodes James, Robert: **Bob Boothby: A Portrait** (Hodder and Stoughton, 1991)

Ritchie, Berry: **Good Company: the Story of Scottish and Newcastle** (James & James (Publishers) Ltd., 1999)

Roberts, Hugh: **The Queen's Diamonds** (Royal Collection Publications, 2012)

Sackville-West, Vita: **The Edwardians** (First published 1930; this edition published by Hogarth Press, 1973)

Simon, Viscount: **Retrospect** (Hutchinson, 1952)

Sitwell, Osbert: **Queen Mary and Others** (Michael Joseph Ltd., 1974)

Sitwell, Osbert: **Great Morning** (Macmillan and Co. Ltd.)

Souhami, Diana: **Mrs Keppel and her Daughter** (HarperCollins 1996; this edition published 1997)

Thorold, Peter: **The Motoring Age: The Automobile and Britain, 1896–1939** (Profile Books, 2003)

Vanderbilt, Cornelius Jnr.: **Queen of the Golden Age: The Fabulous Story of Grace Wilson Vanderbilt** (First published in the USA, 1956; this edition published by George Mann, Maidstone, 1999)

Vickers, Hugo: **Elizabeth The Queen Mother** (Hutchinson, London, 2005)

Williams, Susan: **The People's King: the True Story of the Abdication** (Allen Lane, 2003)

Wilson, A.A.: **The Victorians** (Hutchinson, 2002)

Young, Kenneth (ed.): **The Diaries of Sir Robert Bruce Lockhart, Volume 1 – 1915–1938** (Macmillan, 1973)

Ziegler, Philip (ed): **The Diaries of Lord Louis Mountbatten: 1920–1922 – Tours with the Prince of Wales** (Collins, 1987)

Index